Battle Ready

Conclusion

Judgment

Aaron Hopson

Battle Ready

Conclusion

Judgment

Aaron Hopson

Battle Ready

Conclusion

Judgment

Gems From Joy Ministries

www.battlereadyprayer.com

Prayer Library

http://battlereadyprayer.com/battle-ready-prayers/

To God Be The Glory

Contents

Introduction

Today Christianity is a broad title so vague and inclusive you don't even have to adhere to the Bible or adopt its basic tenants. You simply acknowledge a Creator and have tolerance for your fellow man. In actuality, the Bible states Christianity is a belief system narrowly defined.

Matthew 7:13-14
7:13 "Enter ye in at the strait gate: for wide is the gate, and broad is the way, that leadeth to destruction, and many there be which go in thereat:
7:14 "Because strait is the gate, and narrow is the way, which leadeth unto life, and few there be that find it"

The more the gate widened, the more watered down and distorted the title becomes. Satan has attacked the foundations of Christianity, changing the very identity of what it means to be a Christian. The result is a title so compromised it is in danger of losing its meaning. From the pulpit to the pews, we see people succumbing to this deception. The face of Christianity changes day to day from the messages preached to the lifestyles of professing Christians, and even the core of what we believe. Who could have imagined a day where fundamental beliefs contained in the Bible are disputed?

Christianity has become a religion-saturated with hypocrisy because it appears, we preach one thing and do another. We look and act so identical to the world the title Christian is losing its relevance. Increasingly, the Bible is a reference point as opposed to the final authority, living holy is fanatical and old-fashioned, and the message we present to the world is Jesus' most significant concern is we are happy and prosperous. The more this worldview embraced, we lose our credibility and focus, become self-absorbed and consumed with carnal things, and increasingly avoid sound doctrine.

II Timothy 4:3-4
4:3 "For the time will come when they will not endure sound doctrine; but after their own lusts shall they heap to themselves teachers, having itching ears."
4:4 "And they shall turn away their ears from the truth, and shall be turned unto fables."

This distorted application of Christianity has resulted in a nation increasingly veering away from a genuine belief in God, His statutes and commandments.

What has always held this nation together was a strong dependency on God and the Christian morals and values it was framed. From the formation of our laws to the establishment of biblically based institutions, the morals and values of this nation were shaped with God in mind. We held commonly accepted notions of right and wrong, and the Bible was our moral compass not merely an interesting piece of literature.

These ideas helped America thrive and served as a beacon of light to people all over the world who came here seeking a better life. People of diverse cultural and religious backgrounds migrated to this country, so deeply rooted in Christian traditions and influences, while still having the freedom to practice their own beliefs. Now, these same Christian morals and values are seen as an infringement on the rights of others and banned from our institutions and way of life?

The Bible was our moral code which kept our society from plunging into ungodliness, chaos, and confusion. It protected the sanctity of life, guarded the innocence of children, preserved the family, and taught us how-to walk-in love towards our fellow man. In other words, it prevented us from becoming a godless society, while providing a blueprint to our children that could be passed down from generation to generation. The more we stray away from these values, the faster this nation declines resulting in a society where everything goes, and very little is taboo.

Many of us, by our admission, were defeated and without hope in this world until that glorious day we encountered Jesus Christ, and my story reads the same. I did not have to be taught how to sin; I merely had to be exposed to it. All over the world, there are countless Christians whose lives have been touched by Jesus Christ. The term "Christian" was first used in a place called Antioch to designate the followers of Jesus Christ. The message was simple "salvation through Him, and obedience to His word." They believed in the truth of the gospel and its power to transform the lives of men. Some had witnessed firsthand the life of Jesus Christ while others won through their testimony. The term "Christian" united believers in the faith, declaring Jesus was indeed the Christ, the Anointed One of God.

It was accepted this title came with the responsibility to submit their lives to Him. It was not merely a verbal declaration, but rather a heart commitment to adopt the lifestyle of Jesus Christ and in no way bring reproach upon that worthy name by which they were called. That it may not be said of them which Alexander the Great declared to a soldier of his name noted for being a coward, **"aut nomen, aut mores muta"** – **"Either change thy name or mend thy manners."** (Henry Matthew "Commentary on Acts II." Blue Letter Bible.01 March 1996.)

The message is clear. If we are not going to follow Jesus Christ, then we need to quit calling ourselves Christians. There are too many people today under the false impression the title is what saves them. Early Christians understood the title described the relationship they had with Jesus Christ. It was never meant to be a substitute for living a godly life.

The Christian experience, described in the Bible as an enduring race run with patience, is the collective face we present to the world whether it is good or bad. For some people, Christianity has become nothing more

11

than a placebo used to ease their guilt so they may have a good conscience towards God. It is a license to sin and justification for Heaven. They have no real desire to surrender to God only using religion to fill a void in their lives. This thinking has led to a new definition of Christianity very vague and all-encompassing, having no boundaries or guidelines, and not Biblically based. It has become a title inclusive of every lifestyle as opposed to a lifestyle defined by a title. Christianity is not a religion based on group conformity or a distorted perception of God's love. It is not validated by the views of men, strengthened by opinion polls, or based on consensus, instead; we live by the truth of His Word.

Today, we face increasing challenges as followers of Jesus Christ to conform to the societal definition of Christianity as opposed to staying true to the Biblical meaning. We live in a world which seemingly refutes the very life of Jesus Christ, and Christianity, in its pure form, is under attack. While the battle rages from the outside and within, many Christians are oblivious to the fight. It is a battle against the middle, the lukewarm, and playing on both sides of the fence — the place where Satan dwells under cover of religion, false doctrine, half-heartedness, and carnality.

Revelation 3:14-16
3:14 "And unto the angel of the church of the Laodiceans write; These things saith the Amen, the faithful and true witness, the beginning of the creation of God;"
3:15 "I know thy works, that thou art neither cold nor hot: I would thou wert cold or hot.
3:15 "So then because thou art lukewarm, and neither cold nor hot, I will spue thee out of my mouth."

In understanding the real face of Luciferian worship, the blinders will suddenly fall off, and you will have a greater understanding of the world you are witnessing today. You will understand why it is so important to live without compromise, according to the Bible, no-longer picking and choosing which parts to adhere to and which to ignore. You will understand why many are deceived and why the very fate of Christianity rests in an uncompromised belief Christ is the only way to God. Your eyes will be opened, and the path made crystal clear offering no room for veering or deviation. You will understand why so many people are gravitating away from sound doctrine, and why the media, Hollywood, and entertainment industry is saturated with satanic symbolism and outright disrespect for God. You will understand why a nation that once held God in high esteem is now determined to strip the very thought of God from its institutions and daily life. You will no longer be ignorant of the systematic plan to undermine the institution of marriage and the home. You will discover why people are so willing to abandon established beliefs concerning God, are quick to challenge the divinity of Christ, increasingly see Christians as hateful and intolerant, and in many countries view us as the most hated people in the land.

In the same manner, men once fought to raise the flag; we must now fight to raise the Cross. The Bible compels each of us to take up our cross and follow Him. The cross is our reminder and declaration to the world Christianity is all about Christ, His death, burial, and resurrection. It is about His Word, His teachings, and His commandments. It is about reconciliation to God through Him and Him alone, the

14

power of His blood to wash away sins, a belief in the

virgin birth, and walking in His character and authority.

It is about accepting the Bible as the unadulterated

Word of God and lining up with every letter of every

word on every page and putting God's will before our

own even when it requires us to give up something or

change our ways. It is a declaration we put our trust in

Him and not in man.

Romans 3:-3-4

3:3 "For what if some did not believe? Shall their
unbelief make the faith of God without effect?"
3:4 "God forbid: yea let God be true, but every man a
liar; as it is written, That thou migthest be justified in
thy sayings, and mightest overcome when thou art
judged."

This book is a crash course on how to survive

Christianity in a day full of deception and compromise.

It addresses the foundations of our faith and provides

clarity surrounding what the Bible has to say regarding

the days we are living in.

<u>PRAYER</u>

I thank you, Heavenly Father, for the finished work of the cross. I acknowledge your sacrifice in giving your only Begotten Son, Jesus Christ, to die for my sins and the abundant love you have given to me. I thank you for your plan of redemption that rescued me from my fallen state and the power of the resurrection to bring me into your family. I am bought by the Blood of Jesus, and I surrender my whole heart, mind, body, and soul to you. I accept your precious gift of salvation, and I receive Jesus Christ as my Lord and Savior to guide and direct my life. I acknowledge my faults and shortcomings, and I pray for forgiveness for my sins. In the name of Jesus, I come before you Heavenly Father seeking your face for guidance, wisdom, and instruction to live a life that is pleasing in your sight. I commit to honor and uphold your word and to be sold out and surrendered to the Holy Spirit.

I pray Lord as I read the words of this book that you will give me revelation and understanding that will be fruitful to my life. I understand that your chastening is for my correction and I ask that you convict me in every area of my life that requires change. I stand before you Lord naked in the light of the truth and open my heart and mind to the cleansing power of the unadulterated Word of God to teach me all things. I denounce every tie to the world, ungodly influences and the opinions of men. I declare right now I am free to receive the truth from the word to bring light and revelation into my life. I make a firm commitment to live after the examples of Jesus Christ and take up my cross as a witness to this world. Please help me to overcome my weaknesses and to turn away from all sin. Bless me with courage and give me an honest and sincere heart to approach the future with pure motives and just intentions. I ask all this in the name of Jesus! Amen

<u>Chapter 1 In the Beginning God</u>

The very first verse in the Bible reads:

<u>Genesis 1:1</u> "In the beginning, God created the heaven and the earth."

If there were a verse before that, it would read, **"<u>In the Beginning God,</u>"** The Bible is man's blueprint for life, but before there was ever a Bible there was God. The question asked, "Who was before Him?" and the answer is no one and nothing. He is the Alpha and the Omega, the First and the Last, the Beginning and the End, and if you asked the same question a million times you would be no closer to determining His origin nor could you pinpoint His end. Just consider the vastness of the universe and how little we know about it. Science hasn't even scratched the surface of what indeed exists beyond the reach of our most advanced telescopes and space exploration, but God has given us a record of Himself and everything He wanted us to know about Him is in the Bible.

The Bible is God's blueprint for man. An instruction manual designed to bridge the gap between the limited capacity of our minds and the Almighty God who created all things. The way we cross that bridge is Faith. We believe the Bible is the unadulterated Word of God and every letter, of every word, on every page, is divinely inspired by Him. It is not a mere book of tips and suggestions, but rather the authority for how we live our lives. It is an infallible source of wisdom that has withstood the test of time. It has an answer for every problem and challenge we face in life and has proven to be more reliable than any other basis of information known to man. It contains the very DNA of life and is more accurate than the evening news and contains more knowledge than the internet. It is a living, breathing, and trustworthy blueprint of the universe, which gives us an identity, explains the past, provides accurate and detailed direction and guides us into the future with pinpoint precision. It is light so powerful it eliminates darkness, exposes each thought, and deciphers the deepest intents and motives of the heart. It is a force so dominant it can change the character and content of men, it is so commanding it destroys sickness in the body and mind, and so faithful

it will even save you from destroying yourself.

II Timothy 3:16:17
3:16 "All scripture *is* given by inspiration of God, and
is profitable for doctrine, for reproof, for correction, for
instruction in righteousness:
3:17 "That the man of God may be perfect, throughly
furnished unto all good works.

We are incapable of knowing everything about

God but those things which are for our understanding

He has provided through the Bible.

Revelation 22:13 "I am Alpha and Omega, the
beginning and the end, the first and the last."

Romans 11:33 "O the depth of the riches both of the
wisdom and knowledge of God! how unsearchable *are*
his judgments, and his ways past finding out! "

Deuteronomy 29:29 "The secret *things belong* unto the
LORD our God: but those *things which are* revealed
belong unto us and to our children for ever, that *we* may
do all the words of this law."

The fascinating thing about God is He provided men

with answers before the questions asked. He knew

man's thoughts and even his arrogance. He never

intended for man to be confused He only wanted him to

have faith and belief in Him. He did not want him to follow down the same path as Lucifer, being puffed up in pride and arrogance. As opposed to man trying to bring God down to his level, attempting to contain the majesty of God in the limited space of his mind, or understand that which is beyond his comprehension, God gave men faith to believe in Him.

Revelation 4:11 "Thou art worthy, O Lord, to receive glory and honour and power: for thou hast created all things, and for thy pleasure they are and were created."

Isaiah 29:16 "Surely your turning of things upside down shall be esteemed as the potter's clay: for shall the work say of him that made it, He made me not? or shall the thing framed say of him that framed it, He had no understanding?"

God gave man a revelation of Himself evidenced by His creation, but man chose not to believe, instead, through his intellect and understanding, he created gods to serve and worship, even worshipping himself, leading to foolish and sinful results. Consider a significant passage of scriptures in the book of Romans.

Romans 1:16-24

1:16 "For I am not ashamed of the gospel of Christ: for it is the power of God unto salvation to every one that believeth; to the Jew first, and also to the Greek."

Meaning the sum of God's love is expressed through His Only Begotten Son Jesus Christ, and through Him, we are connected to God. I am bold to proclaim this truth.

1:17 "For therein is the righteousness of God revealed from faith to faith: as it is written, The just shall live by faith."

God's ways are revealed to us by exercising faith in His word, as stated in Hebrews 11:6.

Hebrews 11:6 "But without faith, *it is* impossible to please *him*: for he that cometh to God must believe that he is, and *that* he is a rewarder of them that diligently seek him."

It is impossible to understand God with the natural mind. From start to finish, you can only have a relationship with Him by exercising your faith/belief. You must believe He is who He says He is, and He rewards those who sincerely seek a relationship with Him.

Back to the text in Romans 1:16-24

1:18 "For the wrath of God is revealed from heaven against all ungodliness and unrighteousness of men, who hold the truth in unrighteousness;"

God is not mocked, and His anger demonstrated against those who choose to reject Him and live in rebellion to His will. He is a righteous God, and throughout this book, you will find the love of God and the judgment of God are two opposite sides of the same coin. You can't have one without the other. The love of God is free, but salvation is a choice. Heaven is real, but so is Hell. God is merciful, but He is also just and will avenge all unrighteousness. All of God's creation will bow to Him and recognize His authority.

Romans 14:11-12

14:11 "For it is written, *As* I live, saith the Lord, every knee shall bow to me, and every tongue shall confess to God."
14:12 "So then every one of us shall give account of himself to God."

Back to the main text Romans 1:16-25

1:19 "Because that which may be known of God is manifest in them; for God hath shewed *it* unto them."

When one considers how precisely the sun moves through the sky, not moving to close to destroy life, but never moving too far away to deny us of its heat. Consider the times you have navigated through darkness using the light of the moon even though it's millions of miles away. The beauty of the countless stars which drape the evening sky. When you see the trees or the grass change colors with the seasons, the flowers that bloom and sustain life, the delicate balance of the ecosystem, the roaring of the waves, but still perfectly held in place not exceeding their borders. One has but to open his eyes and consider these things slightly. If you do, you will have no choice but to believe there must be a God!

Psalms 53:1 "The fool hath said in his heart, *There is* no God. Corrupt are they, and have done abominable iniquity: *there is* none that doeth good."

Back to the main text Romans 1:16-24

1:20 "For ever since the world was created, people have seen the earth and sky. Through everything God made, they can see his invisible qualities—his eternal power and divine nature. So they have no excuse for not knowing God."

Scripture tells us God's handiwork is all around us, and we witness His miraculous works daily. His Majesty seen in everything created from the air we breathe to the miracle of life itself. Even the invisible things of God seen in the world around us. We are still discovering things about our universe each day. Think about it, science has found the galaxy extends for billions of miles, and there is still no end in sight. This fact alone demonstrates the foolishness of questioning the existence and absolute power of God. The Bible says we are left with no excuse when it comes to believing in Him. Can you imagine standing before Him and saying, "I did not believe because there was no proof."

1:21 "Because that, when they knew God, they glorified *him* not as God, neither were thankful; but became vain in their imaginations, and their foolish heart was darkened."

So, despite the fact, God gave man a revelation of Himself through the majesty of His creation, he chose not to believe. Instead of accepting the Almighty God, he came up with foolish ideas and attributed His works to other things. Instead of worshipping and giving thanks to the Creator, man created his own gods. In other words, because he lacked the faith to understand God, he rejected the very thought of Him choosing to worship things he could see and control. 1:22 "Professing themselves to be wise, they became fools,"

It's incredible that some of the world's most brilliant men are atheist or intelligent men concluded we came from a bored monkey who got tired of jungle life or smashing rocks that appeared out of nowhere. It's even more amazing how people exercise great faith to believe in this foolishness as opposed to merely accepting the belief in an extraordinary God who created the world from intelligent design. I challenge you to drive across the country waiting for another monkey to change into a man or throw a rock against the wall to see if it produces a frog. You challenge me to show you God, and I will say –BREATHE (It only takes a little faith to believe in God)

1:23 "And changed the glory of the uncorruptible God into an image made like to corruptible man, and to birds, and fourfooted beasts, and creeping things"

So instead of worshipping God, man chose to serve idols, he fashioned from the works of his hands. He worshipped the moon, the stars, things made of wood, silver, and gold, and other idols he created in his mind. He even chose to worship himself.

1:24 "Wherefore God also gave them up to uncleanness through the lusts of their own hearts, to dishonour their own bodies between themselves:"
1:25 "Who changed the truth of God into a lie, and worshipped and served the creature more than the Creator, who is blessed for ever. Amen."

So, God honored man's choice not to worship Him, leaving him to his own devices and an evil and wicked heart. He allowed man to become delusional and his heart grew increasingly dark.

Prayer

Dear Heavenly Father, God, who is supreme in authority and who is in absolute and complete control. The God who created all things and framed the heavens and the earth. We give you exceedingly abundant praise. We thank you for your great wisdom which went into our design, for carefully crafting our minds and orchestrating the many complex and fascinating systems to work together in concert. We thank you we were created with deliberate intent having a specific purpose in mind, and our existence is not the result of coincidence, two rocks smashing together, or an ape who grew bored of living in the jungle. We are not mere organisms aimlessly wandering about in the world hoping to adapt to our environment. We are personally known, uniquely created, and you knew us before we even entered the womb. You are the first and the last, the beginning and the end, and there is no other God but you. Thank you for your majesty in sculpting the heavens and framing the world, for setting each star in the sky, putting the planets in order, and causing the sun and the moon to give their light. You are Awesome,

Lord, and your handiwork seen in all that is made. From the raging of the waves to the grass that covers the earth, the trees that provide shade, and the air we breathe, your sovereignty and power are easily seen. Your Kingdom is endless and your power absolute. You are fascinating, extraordinary, and splendid. You are kind and just and merciful to us. Indeed, we are the product of your mind and the expression of your heart, and we lift you above all things. In Jesus name, we pray. Thank God –Amen

Chapter 2 The Fall

Long before Satan was terrorizing the nations and wreaking havoc on mankind, he was a beautiful angel named Lucifer that dwelt in the very presence of God. Scripture leads us to the conclusion Lucifer was loved by God as evidenced by the position he held in Heaven, and great precision and detail by which he was created. He was a remarkable creature, and his appearance was without spot or blemish. The Bible gives us a very descriptive account of Lucifer before his rebellion and fall. **Ezekiel 28:12** states, "Thou sealest up the sum, full of wisdom, and perfect in beauty," which tells us Lucifer was the total package. The next verse describes his beauty as stunning and breathtaking. He was covered with every precious stone, including the diamond and gold, making him a beautiful sight to behold.

Ezekiel 28:13 "Thou hast been in Eden the garden of God; every precious stone [was] thy covering, the sardius, topaz, and the diamond, the beryl, the onyx, and the jasper, the sapphire, the emerald, and the carbuncle, and gold: the workmanship of thy tabrets and of thy pipes was prepared in thee in the day that thou wast created."

God held nothing back in the design of Lucifer, and the following verse refers to him as the anointed cherub (angel) that covereth who had the privilege of walking up and down God's holy mountain.

Ezekiel 28:14 "Thou [art] the anointed cherub that covereth; and I have set thee [so]: thou wast upon the holy mountain of God; thou hast walked up and down in the midst of the stones of fire.

From this description, it is clear Lucifer did not have two horns and a pitchfork as depicted, but was perfect in the manner of his creation, and given great authority in Heaven. Despite all the love and care God showed Lucifer, he did not reciprocate God's love. Instead of reverencing God as a wonderful creator and being thankful for all he was blessed with, he became lifted in pride and consumed with himself. He became vain in his wisdom, pride filled his heart, and as a result, he no longer sought to be submissive to God, instead; he wanted to be God himself. **Ezekiel 28:15** reads "Thou wast perfect in thy ways from the day that thou wast created, till iniquity was found in thee."

Tragically this iniquity consumed him and led to the downfall of this once beautiful angel that dwelt in the very presence of God.

Isaiah 14:12-15
14:12 "How art thou fallen from heaven, O Lucifer, son of the morning! [how] art thou cut down to the ground, which didst weaken the nations!"
14:13 "For thou hast said in thine heart, I will ascend into heaven, I will exalt my throne above the stars of God: I will sit also upon the mount of the congregation, in the sides of the north:"
14:14 "I will ascend above the heights of the clouds; I will be like the most High."
14:15 "Yet thou shalt be brought down to hell, to the sides of the pit."

The sudden descent of Lucifer is described in the following verses.

Ezekiel 28:16:17;
28:16 "By the multitude of thy merchandise they have filled the midst of thee with violence, and thou hast sinned: therefore I will cast thee as profane out of the mountain of God: and I will destroy thee, O covering cherub, from the midst of the stones of fire.
28:17 "Thine heart was lifted up because of thy beauty, thou hast corrupted thy wisdom by reason of thy brightness: I will cast thee to the ground, I will lay thee before kings, that they may behold thee.

It is essential to understand why and how Lucifer fell because it is the very reason why so many people fall today. Lucifer lost his position in Heaven but not his attributes, wisdom, influence, and beauty. Society has become ripe for his deception as many turn away from God and His commandments. We live in a day and age where we are being bombarded daily with satanic influence and symbolism, lust and perversion, rebellion, and a host of other ungodly spirits. It has gotten so bad he doesn't even have to disguise it anymore; rather, it is seen as vogue and fashionable. Nothing is innocent, and everything is intentional because "there is no middle ground." We live in a state of intense and constant spiritual warfare, and if more people understood who Satan is, they would not foolishly believe they can live on both sides of the fence. The problem for many people is they have no idea they are even in a battle and know very little about who they're fighting. They would understand why everything in life has a purpose, whether it is diabolical or divine, and the importance of guarding what we let in our eyes and ears or the exposure we allow our children. They would understand we are incapable of outsmarting the devil using our wisdom and why every attempt to operate outside of the word of God results in devastating results and consequences. They would recognize why we need a Savior and the importance of surrendering all to Him. They would even understand the difference between merely being religious and having a real and personal relationship with God, neglect and love, and free will and accountability. Learning about Lucifer helps us to develop a healthy fear of God and reverence for His statutes and commandments and brings us to the realization we are nothing without Him. The Bible is our only protection against the clever manipulation and deceptions of Satan as opposed to being a book of unnecessary restrictions and limitations on our liberties as it is often viewed today.

Lucifer's descent from heaven and his reign of terror ultimately end in the lake of fire. Despite the fact he knows his fall is inevitable, he is determined to cause as many people as possible to rebel against the design and plan of God. He already succeeded in drawing away 1/3 of the angels in heaven that chose foolishly to join him in his rebellion. The angels are called stars of heaven in the following verses:

Revelation 12:3-4
12:3 "And there appeared another wonder in heaven; and behold a great red dragon, having seven heads and ten horns, and seven crowns upon his heads."
12:4 "And his tail drew the third part of the stars of heaven, and did cast them to the earth: and the dragon stood before the woman which was ready to be delivered, for to devour her child as soon as it was born."

Revelation 12:7-9
12:7 "And there was war in heaven: Michael and his angels fought against the dragon, and the dragon fought and his angels,"
12:8 "And prevailed not; neither was their place found any more in heaven."
12:9 "And the great dragon was cast out, that old serpent, called the Devil, and Satan, which deceiveth the whole world: he was cast out into the earth, and his angels were cast out with him."

The fact that Satan was able to deceive 1/3 of the angels in heaven to rebel against God speaks volumes concerning the wisdom and influence he possesses. A critical point when we consider the present goal of Satan. The more we are duped into an image of

35

a grotesque beast carrying a pitchfork, the easier it becomes for Satan to carry out his real agenda. When you consider these angels dwelt in the very courts of God and witnessed firsthand His majesty, yet somehow, they were deceived into believing this created being, Satan, would one day ascend above the throne of his creator is incredible. As a result, these angels were sentenced to the same fate as their leader, Satan.

Jude 1:6 "And the angels which kept not their first estate, but left their own habitation, he hath reserved in everlasting chains under darkness unto the judgment of the great day.

II Peter 2:4 "For if God spared not the angels that sinned, but cast [them] down to hell, and delivered [them] into chains of darkness, to be reserved unto judgment;"

It is imperative to understand, for both now and a later discussion concerning the fall of man, it wasn't the love of God that resulted in Satan's banishment from Heaven, nor was it God's love that caused 1/3 of the angels to fall with him in his rebellion. So, when people question, "how can a loving God send a person to hell," you can see the love of God does not send a person to hell. Choosing to follow Satan in his rebellion sends a person to hell.

These rebellious angels are now known as demons and comprise the divisions of Satan's kingdom of darkness. It appears some were immediately cast into the bottomless pit and others will be released for a season during the tribulation period as described in

<u>Revelation 9:1-3;</u>
9:1 "And the fifth angel sounded, and I saw a star fall from heaven unto the earth: and to him was given the key of the bottomless pit."
9:2 "And he opened the bottomless pit; and there arose a smoke out of the pit, as the smoke of a great furnace; and the sun and the air were darkened by reason of the smoke of the pit."
9:3 "And there came out of the smoke locusts upon the earth: and unto them was given power, as the scorpions of the earth have power."

The locust or demonic beings are further described a few scriptures later, and Satan is said to be their king.

9:8 "And they had hair as the hair of women, and their teeth were as [the teeth] of lions."
9:9 "And they had breastplates, as it were breastplates of iron; and the sound of their wings [was] as the sound of chariots of many horses running to battle."

9:10 "And they had tails like unto scorpions, and there were stings in their tails: and their power [was] to hurt men five months."

9:11 "And they had a king over them, [which is] the angel of the bottomless pit, whose name in the Hebrew tongue [is] Abaddon, but in the Greek tongue hath [his] name Apollyon."

Other demons were not sent immediately to the bottomless pit and presently reign with Satan helping him to carry out his demonic agenda against mankind. Satan's demonic hierarchy is explained in the following verse.

Ephesians 6:12 "For we wrestle not against flesh and blood, but against principalities, against powers, against the rulers of the darkness of this world, against spiritual wickedness in high [places]."

The devil is not omnipotent (all powerful) nor is he omniscient (all-knowing), nor is he omnipresent (everywhere at all times). Only God is all powerful, all knowing, and everywhere at all times, thus, Satan must search out his targets based on their vulnerability.

I Peter 5:8 "Be sober, be vigilant; because your adversary the devil, as a roaring lion, walketh about, seeking whom he may devour:"

Due to Satan's limitations, he must rely on an elaborate network of demons to gain information and carry out his diabolical plans. The more people give in to their influence, the more he can work through them to be his agents in the earth. Satan tries very hard to mimic the things of God, and his kingdom is set up very similar to God's kingdom, in a hierarchy. Some demons are more powerful than others, and their assignments vary. Some control individuals, whereas others control geographic regions and territories. Some are responsible for ideologies and belief systems, whereas others control world leaders and political systems.

These demonic beings are real, and their one purpose is to advance Satan's agenda of rebellion. They seek to destroy God's most prized creation, man, by turning him away from God. They work patiently and consistently to accomplish their purpose in many ways. They attack the design and purpose of the family. They bring sickness, disease, and infirmity to destroy the body, cause discouragement, and break the spirit. They labor to tear down lives, break up marriages, draw people into addictions such as alcohol, drugs,

pornography, sexual perversion, and other forms of
bondage. They bring mental instability, including
depression, anxiety, fear, paranoia, and feelings of
doubt, grief, despair, and uncertainty. They destroy our
dreams and leave us hopeless and void of ambition.
They are relentless in their campaign to destroy us and
will not cease until they complete their task. They do
not fight fair and will exploit every vulnerability and
weakness they can to accomplish their goal.

They will kick you when you are down, and if you are
going downhill, they will gladly provide momentum, if
you speak negatively about yourself, they will surely
agree with you, and if you're on the edge of the cliff,
they will conveniently bring a strong wind.

They work extremely hard to cause men to defile
themselves and to distort God's original design,
purpose, and plan by stripping them of their manhood,
influencing them to commit lewd and lascivious acts,
bringing thoughts of torment, violence, and other forms
of deviant behavior. They also use intellect, philosophy,
religion, ideologies, and other forms of deception to
distort the very image of God. In other words, the

primary function of fallen angels is drawing us into rebellion and to entirely dismantle God's purpose for our lives by any means necessary.

I Corinthians 4:3-4
4:3 "But if our gospel be hid, it is hid to them that are lost:"
4:4 "In whom the god of this world hath blinded the minds of them which believe not, lest the light of the glorious gospel of Christ, who is the image of God, should shine unto them."

Luke 8:30 "And Jesus asked him, saying, What is thy name? And he said, Legion: because many devils were entered into him."

The Fall of Man

Genesis 1:26-28; 2:7
1:26 "And God said, Let us make man in our image, after our likeness: and let them have dominion over the fish of the sea, and over the fowl of the air, and over the cattle, and over all the earth, and over every creeping thing that creepeth upon the earth.
1:27 "So God created man in his [own] image, in the image of God created he him; male and female created he them.
1:28 "And God blessed them, and God said unto them, Be fruitful, and multiply, and replenish the earth, and subdue it: and have dominion over the fish of the sea, and over the fowl of the air, and over every living thing that moveth upon the earth.
2:7 "And the LORD God formed man [of] the dust of the ground, and breathed into his nostrils the breath of life; and man became a living soul.

God created man from the dust of the ground and breathed life into his nostrils, causing him to become a living soul. Like a baby in a mother's womb, the woman came out of the body of man. She was not a separate and distinct creation, rather a part of the man. The scripture says, "in the image of God created He him; male and female created He them." Man was made after the likeness of God, and from the beginning, He wanted the man and the woman to be one just as He is one with the Son.

John 1:1-2
1:1 "In the beginning was the Word, and the Word was with God, and the Word was God.
1:2 "The same was in the beginning with God"

Just as the Word manifested in the flesh to accomplish God's purpose in the earth; likewise, the woman was manifested for a purpose. Jesus Christ was manifested to become the Savior for all men and the woman to be the companion and help meet for man.

John 1:14 "And the Word was made flesh, and dwelt among us, (and we beheld his glory, the glory as of the only begotten of the Father,) full of grace and truth.

Genesis 2:18 ; 21-22
2:18 "And the LORD God said, *It is* not good that the man should be alone; I will make him an help meet for him."
2:21 "And the LORD God caused a deep sleep to fall upon Adam, and he slept: and he took one of his ribs, and closed up the flesh instead thereof;"
2:22 "And the rib, which the LORD God had taken from man, made he a woman, and brought her unto the man."

Nothing about God's design is random or coincidental, nor is He merely making this up as He goes. Nature itself bears witness to His design. He has a very deliberate and intentional rationale for everything He does. The same way He separated them He made way for them to fit perfectly together, proving when He created man and woman, He had a specific function and purpose in mind. On this idea hinges the entire battle between God and Satan. Satan's agenda is to distort, warp, dismantle, undermine, alter, and destroy God's design to replace it with his own. A reality very evident in society today, as he attempts to use anything under his authority to accomplish this goal.

Adam and Eve shared a common purpose while having two very distinct roles in achieving that purpose. They were designed to be mutually dependent, not equal, and both were needed to replenish the earth and bring it into subjection. The first man, Adam, had a definite role given to him by God before Eve was formed. Likewise, Eve was given a different role. Adam was placed in the Garden of Eden and instructed to dress and keep it. He was God's ambassador in the garden. He was the caretaker, protector, and guardian of the garden. It was Adam who named everything in the garden, Adam who God spoke with in the cool of the day, and Adam who would later bear the brunt of the responsibility stemming from their transgression. One day God looked upon him and decided it was not good for him to be alone. He placed him in a deep sleep and removed one of his ribs in which he formed the female, Eve, to be his helpmeet or companion.

Genesis 2: 8; 15
2:8 "And the LORD God planted a garden eastward in Eden; and there he put the man whom he had formed. 2:15 "And the LORD God took the man, and put him into the garden of Eden to dress it and to keep it."

God established the covenant of marriage with Adam and Eve proving he did not want them to simply live together. The covenant of marriage holds more considerable significance than a few words witnessed by a ceremony and a piece of paper. Biblical marriage is a trilateral relationship between the man, his wife, and God. Spiritually speaking, marriage joins the woman back into the body of the man, causing them to be one flesh again in unity with God. From out of the man the woman came and through marriage, she is returned to him completing the original design and purpose of God they be one spiritually. In God's eyes, sex is more than a pleasurable experience; it is a spiritual union in which the woman becomes one again with the man. It is not a matter of preference but purpose and design. It is a spiritual process God created and controls. If you believe the Bible, it is clear man can elect to change the definition of marriage, but he can never alter the spiritual significance and covenant with God because he is not the architect of its design.

Genesis 2:24
2:24 "Therefore shall a man leave his father and his mother, and shall cleave unto his wife: and they shall be one flesh."

Matthew 19:4-6
19:4 "And he answered and said unto them, Have ye not read, that he which made *them* at the beginning made them male and female,"
19:5 "And said, For this cause shall a man leave father and mother, and shall cleave to his wife: and they twain shall be one flesh?"
19:6 "Wherefore they are no more twain, but one flesh. What therefore God hath joined together, let not man put asunder."

The Bible states to engage in sexual activity outside of the covenant of marriage is to sin against the body by opening your spirit to something other than God. It is a reciprocal exchange granting access to your spirit to something other than God. The Bible likens it to joining one's self to a harlot and committing spiritual adultery. In other words, sex is a spiritual process in which two become one, so by deviating from God's design opens the door to unintended consequences.

I Corinthians 6:15-18
6:15 "Know ye not that your bodies are the members of Christ? shall I then take the members of Christ, and make *them* the members of an harlot? God forbid."
6:16 "What? know ye not that he which is joined to an harlot is one body? for two, saith he, shall be one flesh."
6:17 "But he that is joined unto the Lord is one spirit."
6:18 "Flee fornication. Every sin that a man doeth is without the body; but he that committeth fornication sinneth against his own body."

James 4:4 "Ye adulterers and adulteresses, know ye not that the friendship of the world is enmity with God? whosoever therefore will be a friend of the world is the enemy of God."

Given man was created in the image of God, his character is rooted and grounded in love, and it is clear from his design, God did not want him following the same course as Lucifer. Lucifer's downfall was pride as a result of falling in love with himself. He became fascinated with his beauty, impressed by his design, in awe of his talents and abilities, and mesmerized by his wisdom. It was intoxicating and the more he admired himself, the more he gave over to pride and iniquity, which resulted in rebellion and turning away from God. Marriage is a natural exchange in which the man shares his love with the woman, and his desire is for her and not himself. It produces comfort, stability, and security for the entire family. He is a spiritual covering for his home and instructed to love his wife the same way Christ loved the church and gave His life for it. He provides for her, builds up her self-esteem, protects her, unconditionally loves her, covers her in prayer, and by speaking the Word of God over her life. He stands between her and darkness and presents her before Christ holy and without blemish.

If men had loved their wives, the way God intended we would have never witnessed the breakdown of the family like we see today, and submission would be easy. Imagine submitting to someone who has been supernaturally empowered to love you with all his heart. Godly submission requires the man and the woman to first be submitted to Him and is based on love, not power. The purpose of submission is to align the spiritual body with God. It is the vehicle in which the man demonstrates the character and love of God to His family, keeping them from the rebellion that is in the world.

Ephesians 5:22-31

5:22 "Wives, submit yourselves unto your own husbands, as unto the Lord.

5:23 "For the husband is the head of the wife, even as Christ is the head of the church: and he is the savior of the body.

5:24 "Therefore as the church is subject unto Christ, so [let] the wives [be] to their own husbands in everything."

5:25 "Husbands, love your wives, even as Christ also loved the church, and gave himself for it;"

5:26 "That he might sanctify and cleanse it with the washing of water by the word,"

5:27 "That he might present it to himself a glorious church, not having spot, or wrinkle, or any such thing; but that it should be holy and without blemish."

5:28 "So ought men to love their wives as their own bodies. He that loveth his wife loveth himself."

5:29 "For no man ever yet hated his own flesh; but nourisheth and cherisheth it, even as the Lord the church:"
5:30 "For we are members of his body, of his flesh, and of his bones."
5:31 "For this cause shall a man leave his father and mother, and shall be joined unto his wife, and they two shall be one flesh."

We should all recognize the more profound spiritual conflict here because when it comes to marriage, one could just say, "I don't believe the Bible, nor do I choose to accept what it says." However, Satan is not out to change opinions; he seeks to change the very institution/design of God and replace it with his own. His design is based on the philosophy "do as thou wilt shall be the whole of the law." In other words, man is a god and free to live as he desires without being subject to the laws of an unseen God. Satan understands the only way to accomplish his goal of absolutely corrupting and destroying man is to liberate his mind from submission to the Most High God. In other words, he must draw men into his rebellion the same way he drew 1/3 of the angels in Heaven. Rebellion is operating outside of the design of God.

Romans 1:26-27

1:26 "For this cause God gave them up unto vile affections: for even their women did change the natural use into that which is against nature:
1:27 "And likewise also the men, leaving the natural use of the woman, burned in their lust one toward another; men with men working that which is unseemly, and receiving in themselves that recompense of their error which was meet."

The previous scriptures speak to design. In other words, there is a natural design. Verse 1:26 states "that which is against nature," and verse 1:27 states "that which is unseemly," meaning you are forcing something to fit where it was not designed, thus altering the intent. This is the basis in which we advocate the institution of marriage between a man and a woman. It is a matter of God's sovereign design, plan, and purpose. Not based on political affiliation, opinion, two people loving each other, or personal preference, nor is it the result of hate, discrimination, or being insensitive towards the rights of others. We choose to accept the design of God, as expressed in the Bible.

God had blessed Adam in every area of his life. He was his source of being in that he breathed life into his nostrils. His source of joy in that Adam had no

51

sorrow, heartaches, or pain. His source of health in that Adam was not touched by sickness, disease, or infirmity. His source for companionship in that He blessed Adam with Eve, his source of comfort in that He fellowshipped with him in the cool of the day, and his source of peace in that Adam was free of depression, fear, anxiety, or worry. God gave him the power to exercise dominion and authority over all the works of His hands. The only thing God required of Adam was his obedience.

God had given Adam every tree in the garden to eat from except the tree of the knowledge of good and evil. God told him he was forbidden to eat from that tree and warned him if he ever did, he would surely die. God's instruction had nothing to do with Adam's personal preferences, nor was it an infringement on Adam's rights. It was a result of His sovereign plan and design. There are those today who would probably claim God was intolerant or He hated Adam because He told him he couldn't eat from that tree.

Genesis 2:16-17
2:16 "And the LORD God commanded the man, saying, Of every tree of the garden thou mayest freely eat:
2:17 "But of the tree of the knowledge of good and evil, thou shalt not eat of it: for in the day that thou eatest thereof thou shalt surely die."

This limitation revealed the greatest attribute Adam possessed, which was the gift of choice and free will. God gave Adam the right to choose and counseled Him on making the right choice. The right to choose set Adam apart from all of God's creatures because it gave him the ability to reciprocate God s love. True love is not the result of force or coercion, but the product of choice in the face of other options. It is evident God was creating a family who would choose to love and obey Him and spend eternity with Him.

Despite all the many blessings Adam received, there was still another path he could choose to follow. Satan's rebellion did not end when cast out of Heaven. He had already succeeded in drawing away 1/3 of the angelic host, and now his eyes were set on man. Even though this once mighty angel who walked in the very mountain of God now lurked in the Garden of Eden, he was never intended to pose any threat to man. Adam knew Satan was present because he had authority over the garden and everything in it, including him. It was Adam who named every creature in the garden, including the serpent. God put all things under Adam's feet, and his instructions were to protect and keep the garden, but the presence of Satan presented him an alternative to following God.

Satan tempted Eve using the same tools of deception which led to his demise, which were lust and pride. He led Eve to believe she could be more than what God created her to be even becoming a god herself. He convinced her using the same premise he still uses today "Do what thou wilt," which is the fallen nature of man. It is a philosophy built on following one's preferences as opposed to God's design. The more she entertained his logic, the more attractive the idea became, and her heart and mind were opened. It is a philosophy based on no restraints and self-gratification as opposed to obedience and submission.

Genesis 3:1-5
3:1 "Now the serpent was more subtil than any beast of the field which the LORD God had made. And he said

unto the woman, Yea, hath God said, Ye shall not eat of every tree of the garden?

3:2 "And the woman said unto the serpent, We may eat of the fruit of the trees of the garden:

3:3 "But of the fruit of the tree which [is] in the midst of the garden, God hath said, Ye shall not eat of it, neither shall ye touch it, lest ye die.

3:4 "And the serpent said unto the woman, Ye shall not surely die:

3:5 "For God doth know that in the day ye eat thereof, then your eyes shall be opened, and ye shall be as gods, knowing good and evil."

Instead of protecting his wife from the influence of Satan and enforcing the will of God, Adam let his guard down and made a conscious decision to join Eve in turning away from His commandments. The instant Adam took a bite of the forbidden fruit, spiritual and physical death was the result. Immediately, he was thrust headlong into Satan's rebellion.

Genesis 3:6-7
3:6 "And when the woman saw that the tree [was] good for food, and that it [was] pleasant to the eyes, and a tree to be desired to make [one] wise, she took of the fruit thereof, and did eat, and gave also unto her husband with her; and he did eat.

3:7 "And the eyes of them both were opened, and they knew that they [were] naked; and they sewed fig leaves together, and made themselves aprons."

Instantly, Adam's authority transferred to Satan, and he became the god of this world or one who possesses authority. The Bible is clear concerning Satan's power in this world.

Romans 6:16 "Know ye not, that to whom ye yield yourselves servants to obey, his servants ye are to whom ye obey; whether of sin unto death, or of obedience unto righteousness?

II Corinthians 4:3-4
4:3 "But if our gospel be hid, it is hid to them that are lost:"
4:4 "In whom the god of this world hath blinded the minds of them which believe not, lest the light of the glorious gospel of Christ, who is the image of God, should shine unto them."

Adam was stripped of his dominion and authority, and from that moment forward, all of mankind proceeding from his seed inherited the curse of sin, which is sickness, poverty, and death. This event marked the fall of man and all the rules changed, and the authority God had given him was transferred to Satan, making him the god of this world. The destiny of man would never be the same. His struggle, his ultimate fate, his understanding, his relationship and fellowship with

God, all changed. He became a slave to his flesh and subjected to his fallen nature and the influence of Satan.

Genesis 3:17-19

3:17 "And unto Adam he said, Because thou hast hearkened unto the voice of thy wife, and hast eaten of the tree, of which I commanded thee, saying, Thou shalt not eat of it: cursed [is] the ground for thy sake; in sorrow shalt thou eat [of] it all the days of thy life;
3:18 "Thorns also and thistles shall it bring forth to thee; and thou shalt eat the herb of the field;
3:19 "In the sweat of thy face shalt thou eat bread, till thou return unto the ground; for out of it wast thou taken: for dust thou [art], and unto dust shalt thou return."

James 1:13-15

1:13 "Let no man say when he is tempted, I am tempted of God: for God cannot be tempted with evil, neither tempteth he any man:
1:14 "But every man is tempted, when he is drawn away of his own lust, and enticed.
1:15 "Then when lust hath conceived, it bringeth forth sin: and sin, when it is finished, bringeth forth death."

Sin began the moment Adam veered away from the commandment of God. Sin had not previously existed in Adam, the choice to sin did, and once he exercised his choice, it opened the door for sin and rebellion. Yet, another example of Satan's great wisdom and influence. He had succeeded once again in what he thought was a punishing blow to God, but God had already devised another plan to put Satan under man's feet once again. Satan underestimated the magnitude of God's love and just how much He was willing to sacrifice for man. God had a solution for man's disobedience before Adam ever thought about biting the fruit. Later, we shall discuss "Gods Perfect Plan, the Only Hope for Fallen Man."

I Corinthians 2:9 "But as it is written, Eye hath not seen, nor ear heard, neither have entered into the heart of man, the things which God hath prepared for them that love him."

Ephesians 1:3-4
1:3 "Blessed *be* the God and Father of our Lord Jesus Christ, who hath blessed us with all spiritual blessings in heavenly *places* in Christ:"
1:4 "According as he hath chosen us in him before the foundation of the world, that we should be holy and without blame before him in love:

Now when you consider the price and consequences of sin do you understand why Adam would not have been judging his wife, insensitive towards his wife, or being hateful or intolerant for pointing out the instructions God had given them? Well, that's precisely how Christians are viewed today when they point out Biblical truths. Truths you are free to receive or reject just as Adam and Eve were given that choice. The gospel is the proclamation of truth in the face of competing ideas, rebellion, free will, and choice. Satan seeks to silence this truth by attacking those who have faith to believe in it. These attacks will intensify in the days to come but take comfort in the words of our Saviour Jesus Christ;

John 16:33 "These things I have spoken unto you, that in me ye might have peace. In the world ye shall have tribulation: but be of good cheer; I have overcome the world

<u>Prayer</u>

Praises be to the All Mighty and Powerful God, The Rock of our Salvation, The Everlasting Father who holds the universe in His hands. The Omnipotent One who is all powerful and keeps the necks of His enemies under His feet. In the Name of Jesus and the power of His Blood, we rebuke and bind every demonic being assigned to us. We rebuke and bind all manner of sickness, disease, and infirmity, right now in Jesus name. In the name of Jesus and the power of His Blood, we bind all forms of discouragement, distortions of the truth, depression, mental instability, hopelessness, anxiety, and false ideologies and beliefs. We bind every attempt of Satan to tear apart or bring dysfunction into our marriages, relationships, and homes right now in Jesus name. In the name of Jesus and the power of His Blood, we exercise the authority we have been given through Him to break the vices of drugs, pornography, sexual perversion, gender confusion, alcohol and drug addictions, and any rebellious spirits operating outside of the design and plan of God. In the name of Jesus, we render every demonic attack null and void and come against any traces of fear, paranoia, doubt, grief, and uncertainty. Close every door of attack and vulnerability in our lives and drive back the relentless waves of demonic maneuvers and strategies designed to exploit perceived weakness, for we are covered by the Blood of Jesus and the knowledge and revelation of His word. We are His people, divinely protected by Him and the Heavenly Host of Angels He has assigned to war on our behalf. That our Angels excel in strength and fulfill every purpose of God in our lives. In Jesus name, we pray. Thank God – Amen

What Really Happened in the Garden?

Within **Genesis 3:1-5** lie two diabolically opposed versions of the events which transpired in the Garden of Eden. On these opposing beliefs rest two very different trains of thought that will ultimately determine the fate of both camps who have bet the farm their version is correct. The stakes could not be higher, and the result is either eternal life in the Kingdom of God or Lucifer will reign supreme over all creation.

As Christians, we are aware of the battle waging since Lucifer's rebellion in Heaven and subsequent fall. We recognize the spiritual warfare which exists today as Satan makes one last desperate attempt to thwart the design, purpose, and plan of God, which ultimately forecasts his fate in the lake of fire. Within his twisted logic and flawed thinking, he believes by corrupting man and turning him away from God; he can change his destiny. He recognizes the deep seeded love God has for His most prized creation and hopes man's rebellion will orchestrate a kingdom of his own.

Psalm 8:3-6

8:3 "When I consider thy heavens, the work of thy fingers, the moon, and the stars, which thou hast ordained;

8:4 "What is man, that thou art mindful of him? and the son of man, that thou visitest him?

8:5 "For thou hast made him a little lower than the angels, and hast crowned him with glory and honour.

8:6 "Thou madest him to have dominion over the works of thy hands; thou hast put all [things] under his feet:"

Satan is not all knowing and all powerful, so although he should understand how the story is going to end, he believes he can change his fate. The Bible is clear on this point dating back to his attempts to destroy the coming Messiah at birth or his greatest blunder of all moving men to crucify the Lord Jesus Christ. Satan's downfall is he incapable of figuring out the mind of God and His ultimate plan for man.

I Corinthians 2:7-8

2:7 "But we speak the wisdom of God in a mystery, *even* the hidden *wisdom*, which God ordained before the world unto our glory:"

2:8 "Which none of the princes of this world knew: for had they known *it*, they would not have crucified the Lord of glory."

I included this chapter because unless you understand both schools of thought, nothing happening in the world today will make sense to you.

Lucifer The Light Bearer

For most people, it's tough to believe an intelligent person would choose to worship the devil. We relegate such nonsense to certain types of extreme rock music we can tune out, random acts of psychotic serial killers, or the out of touch occultist group sacrificing animals and participating in orgies. Regardless of your view, most people hold some form of Hollywood manufactured picture of Satan holding a pitchfork while laughing in the most sinister and frightening way. A perception reinforced by horror films depicting very base and senseless violence and other dark images.

Indeed, all these things can be manifestations of satanic influence; however; they rank very low on the totem pole when discovering the real face and nature of Satan. He indeed derives great pleasure and satisfaction from seeing man reduced to his most vile and animalistic form. He thrives on the pain, misery, and suffering of man and has always hated his existence. He is the father of every foul, violent, cruel, vile, debased, and vulgar act, however; this is not the deceptive and influential face of Satan, causing countless people to fall. These are mere symptoms of a more prominent disease. His ultimate goal and plan for man is rebellion against God defacing the very image and likeness of his creator and enslaving him to an eternity of pain, torment, and suffering. Satan is not seeking mere servitude; he is seeking revenge by poisoning the souls of the ones God loves most. The more lives he can destroy, the better. Many people who serve and worship Satan, whether directly or indirectly, see him in an entirely different light. By manifesting himself in various forms, he is welcomed into the lives and homes of his faithful. This is coupled with an ideology of love that embraces man's fallen nature as opposed to redeeming it.

II Corinthians 11:14 "And no marvel; for Satan himself is transformed into an angel of light.

Most reasonable people would never follow him if they understood his true nature; instead; they follow him because he manifests himself as a friend. He is the great deceiver and a master at deception and disguise, and the advantage he has is there are so many ways to get it wrong, but only one way to get it right.

Matthew 7:13-14
7:13 "Enter ye in at the strait gate: for wide *is* the gate, and broad *is* the way, that leadeth to destruction, and many there be which go in thereat:"
7:14 "Because strait *is* the gate, and narrow *is* the way, which leadeth unto life, and few there be that find it."

The real face of Satan takes on a very different form manifested at the highest levels of position and power. The power behind the power who have submitted to Satan's authority. No blood, no gore. The face causing seemingly sane people to accept the belief Satan is god and leads gifted and talented men and women to pay the ultimate price for worldly success, which is their souls. They come in many different shapes and forms ranging in names, organization affiliations, secret societies, titles, and belief systems. They are the heads of state, government officials, wealthy businessmen and women, influential voices, powerful political figures, and the movers and shakers of this world. They are your favorite athletes, movie stars, radio/TV personalities, and celebrities. They are doctors, lawyers, teachers, pastors, law enforcement officers, and the church-going couple next door. They look very ordinary, attend church and worship services, perform humanitarian acts, sit on school boards, and coach little league. Many have tremendous wealth, fame, and influence owning and controlling the highest levels of media, including entertainment, sports, news, and Hollywood.

With such an exhaustive list, you may be saying to yourself "that list includes everybody," and you are correct. The question is not "Who serves Satan," rather; "Who doesn't serve him anymore." There is a time in all our lives; Satan is in the mirror. When Adam sinned, everyone born after him was shaped in iniquity and born into sin. In other words, we come into this world in rebellion and under the influence and control of Satan. The truth is you don't choose to serve Satan; you decide not to serve him. The choice God has given us is whether we will choose to be born again through His

Only Begotten Son Jesus Christ. It is critical to understand God loves us the way He created us before the fall, not the way we are born into this world.

Romans 5:12 "Wherefore, as by one man sin entered into the world, and death by sin; and so death passed upon all men, for that all have sinned:"

THE OTHER VERSION OF THE GARDEN OF EDEN

As I stated previously, Satan is driven by numbers. He has a very top to bottom approach when it comes to cultivating disciples, destroying homes and biblical institutions, and leading the masses away from the knowledge and understanding of God. You could even say he is the incumbent in this race, which gives him a perceived advantage. He is the god of this world and appeals to our deepest desires and pleasures. He influences much of what we see on television, what we hear on the radio and the messages in our entertainment industry. He shapes the popular morals and values of the day, often, under cover of political correctness.

Romans 12:2 "And be not conformed to this world: but be ye transformed by the renewing of your mind, that ye may prove what *is* that good, and acceptable, and perfect, will of God."

II Corinthians 4:4 "In whom the god of this world hath blinded the minds of them which believe not, lest the light of the glorious gospel of Christ, who is the image of God, should shine unto them."

The ideas are carefully and meticulously formed at the top and pushed down to the masses, but why? Why are so many willing to be used by him?

To fully understand the "why," you must consider a vastly different version of what happened in the Garden of Eden. A version of the story as twisted as the words spoken into the ears of Eve by the serpent.

Genesis 3:1-5
3:1 "Now the serpent was more subtil than any beast of the field which the LORD God had made. And he said unto the woman, Yea, hath God said, Ye shall not eat of every tree of the garden?
3:2 "And the woman said unto the serpent, We may eat of the fruit of the trees of the garden:
3:3 "But of the fruit of the tree which [is] in the midst of the garden, God hath said, Ye shall not eat of it, neither shall ye touch it, lest ye die.
3:4 "And the serpent said unto the woman, Ye shall not surely die:
3:5 "For God doth know that in the day ye eat thereof, then your eyes shall be opened, and ye shall be as gods, knowing good and evil."

The reason Lucifer is referred to as "The Light Bearer" by those who possess the knowledge is his followers view him as a friend seeking to liberate man from the tyranny of an unjust God. Many people have heard of secret societies such as the Illuminati who derive their root from the word "Illuminate." Illuminate means to be intellectually or spiritually enlightened. They hold firm to the belief they have been illuminated with secret knowledge the masses do not have. They see it as their duty to control the wealth and power of the world because the masses are incapable of governing themselves. They see them like blind sheep needing to be controlled for their good. They wholeheartedly believe the enslaved masses are useless and left to themselves, will overpopulate, consume the world's resources and destroy the environment. They believe by stripping society of its dependency on God; they will ultimately create a utopia. A society in which "Do as thou wilt," is the order of the day and man no longer foolishly depends on God.

They believe that moment in the garden changed everything. It was a wakeup call for man when

70

Lucifer came to Eve to impart hidden knowledge to her. He knew Eve did not possess the knowledge derived from the tree of good and evil, but he did. Remember he was once in Heaven and walked in the very courts of God. He was aware of both good and evil and knew the significance of this tree the Lord commanded Adam and Eve not to eat.

Genesis 3:1 "Now the serpent was more subtil than any beast of the field which the LORD God had made. And he said unto the woman, Yea, hath God said, Ye shall not eat of every tree of the garden?

Lucifer already knew the answer but was drawing attention to the one restriction God had placed on man. Lucifer came to befriend man and share the knowledge of his full potential. His followers believe he did not fall from heaven; instead; he rose from the bondage of subjection to God. To them, he is the Bright Morning Star, bearer of light and truth. The secret he so desperately wanted man to know was that **man was a god**.

3:2 "And the woman said unto the serpent, We may eat of the fruit of the trees of the garden:

71

3:3 "But of the fruit of the tree which [is] in the midst of the garden, God hath said, Ye shall not eat of it, neither shall ye touch it, lest ye die.
3:4 "And the serpent said unto the woman, Ye shall not surely die:
3:5 "For God doth know that in the day ye eat thereof, then your eyes shall be opened, and ye shall be as gods, knowing good and evil."

Eve responds, "we have a right to eat of every tree just not this one, for if we eat of that tree, we shall die." Lucifer then reveals the gnosis or secret knowledge of the tree, which directly contradicted God's instructions.

Once again, this is a Luciferian perspective

Lucifer revealed to Eve a hidden truth God maliciously kept from her. A secret he concealed to keep man enslaved in darkness. Lucifer came to free man from obscurity, which was the essence of his rebellion. He recognized his greatness and no longer wanted to be limited by God.

Isaiah 14:13-14
14:13 "For thou hast said in thine heart, I will ascend into heaven, I will exalt my throne above the stars of God: I will sit also upon the mount of the congregation, in the sides of the north:"
14:14 "I will ascend above the heights of the clouds; I will be like the most High."

Despite the fact, mature Christians, know this rebellion was an utter failure, those who believe they have been enlightened view it as Lucifer's greatest success. The moment he received the gnosis he did not have to be subjected to God because He was a God himself. The moment of illumination in which he was liberated and set free. To his followers, he is a revolutionary and victory comes with struggle. Although they recognize he may have lost a minor battle in Heaven, they believe he will ultimately win the war. Throughout history, men have fought against their oppressors for independence despite the hefty price they had to pay. They passionately believe victory is achieved when the light comes on and the masses rise against their captors, no longer accepting tyranny.

3:5 "For God doth know that in the day ye eat thereof, then your eyes shall be opened, and ye shall be as gods, knowing good and evil."

In this instance, Lucifer reveals the ultimate truth to man that God has hidden this knowledge from him because He seeks to keep him enslaved and under His control. He explains to Eve she is indeed a god and equal to the gods. The phrase used is you shall be as gods, meaning you shall be like one of us. They believe this revelation is the key to unlocking the true nature of man, which is to be self-reliant and free to live with no restrictions — known as The Law of Thelema.

Lucifer knew the authority God had given to man because he was also under man's authority. Remember he once had tremendous power, position, and honor in heaven. He fully knew the consequences of disobedience and rebellion and understood the only way he could strip man of his authority was man made a conscious choice to rebel against God. Again, this is the agenda he has used to shape our world. When I use the term "world," I am referring to those who possess the gnosis. The institutions and people behind the power who make decisions for us each day. Those who believe they must free us from the evil that is God.

Genesis 3:6 "And when the woman saw that the tree *was* good for food, and that it *was* pleasant to the eyes, and a tree to be desired to make *one* wise, she took of the fruit thereof, and did eat, and gave also unto her husband with her; and he did eat."

The moment Eve entertained or made a conscious decision to receive what Satan was saying, the process of lust and temptation began. The same playbook he continues to use today. Whatever the Bible says, Satan will pose the question, "Did God really say that?'

James 1:13-15
1:13 "Let no man say when he is tempted, I am tempted of God: for God cannot be tempted with evil, neither tempteth he any man:
1:14 "But every man is tempted, when he is drawn away of his own lust, and enticed.
1:15 "Then when lust hath conceived, it bringeth forth sin: and sin, when it is finished, bringeth forth death."

As Christians, we know the minute Eve entertained Satan, lust conceived, and she and Adam were drawn into rebellion. The result was spiritual death, and the process of natural death began. It is vital to understand from the minute we are born into this world; Satan seeks to blind us from the truth. To his followers, this marked the moment of illumination as Adam and Eve received the gnosis of who they were. They compare God to a slave master who rules over his subjects by keeping them in a state of ignorance. They

75

determined to no longer be enslaved and seized the opportunity to be enlightened and released from the ignorance that had them bound. Ignorance was their captor as long as they didn't know the truth. In history, a slave caught with a book could be beaten severely or even put to death. The institution thrived on the slave's ignorance to maintain dominance over them. The master's greatest fear was if they ever discovered the truth of their potential, they would rise and overthrow him.

The problem with mankind, according to the enlightened ones, is the masses are still in darkness and refuse to leave the plantation. They believe the evil that is Christianity has taught them to love their oppressor. They feel the masses are too lazy and dependent to discover the gnosis of whom they are, clinging to self-imposed vices such as religion because they are too stupid to think for themselves. They can't understand how they willingly subject themselves to a cruel God who restricts their freedom and holds them back from realizing their desires and reaching their true potential.

The truth is, although they despise the pathetic masses, they also need us to accomplish their goal. They believe in the human spirit like King Nimrod when he attempted to build the tower of Babel to reach unto Heaven. They recognize the power of unification, be it by consent or conquest. Therefore, they want a New World Order comprised of a One World Government and One World Religion where Lucifer is God. They are saying to God, "You stopped us last time, but now we are more numerous and powerful, and won't be stopped again." In their mind, through technology, we are no longer separated by language or geography and can once again challenge God. They have confidence in the fact today we can accomplish things we never imagined, even cloning life, and if we all rise together, there is nothing we can't achieve. Even God acknowledged the power of unification, stating when the people are one, they can accomplish anything they set out to do.

THE TOWER OF BABEL ALL OVER AGAIN!

Genesis 11:4-9

11:4 "And they said, Go to, let us build us a city and a tower, whose top *may reach* unto heaven; and let us make us a name, lest we be scattered abroad upon the face of the whole earth."

11:5 "And the LORD came down to see the city and the tower, which the children of men builded."

11:6 "**And the LORD said, Behold, the people *is* one, and they have all one language; and this they begin to do: and now nothing will be restrained from them, which they have imagined to do.**"

11:7 "Go to, let us go down, and there confound their language, that they may not understand one another's speech."

11:8 "So the LORD scattered them abroad from thence upon the face of all the earth: and they left off to build the city."

11:9 "Therefore is the name of it called Babel; because the LORD did there confound the language of all the earth: and from thence did the LORD scatter them abroad upon the face of all the earth."

They believe freedom is achieved by freeing the minds of the masses from the tyranny of God by indulging the flesh where the Bible says to crucify it. In satisfying the flesh, we are making a conscious choice to continue in rebellion, biting the forbidden fruit of liberation, freeing our minds from the restrictions and fear placed on us by God. This rebellion is the doorway to enlightenment, and the more the flesh defiled, the more our spirits set free. The more we entertain darkness and depravity, the more we satisfy our deepest sexual fantasies and perversions, the more we deface and defile our bodies, and the more we celebrate sin, we are released from captivity and free to receive and live in the gnosis we are as gods, restrained by nothing and no one. It is a selfish, loveless, philosophy built on self-indulgence and unrestrained appetites. Take what you will, do what you will, have what you will, and consume your lust until your cup is filled, for this is man's right. The reason why we see the dramatic rise in sexual orientations and genders is labeling or acknowledging behavior is a form of affirmation by removing the stigma associated with it. Soon, it will be acceptable to have sex with anything moving if that's what satisfies your desire. They will create a new category and name to legitimize the behavior and accommodate your choice.

The masses are deceived into believing they have to agree with the plan when all that's required is they live according to it. When Nimrod built the tower, the masses weren't included in the planning they merely supplied the labor and the bricks. There is no middle ground, and if you live for Satan, he is your god, whether, you acknowledge him or not. The more we veer from God's commandments, the more we assist the enlightened ones to accomplish their objectives. The more bombarded with lust and entertained by drama, the more oblivious we become. The more we refuse to stand for biblical institutions and are silent on matters like marriage, abortion, and neglect the poor, we play right into their hands. The more we blindly follow celebrities who blatantly endorse satanism bringing rebellion into our homes, and the more we fail to protect the innocence of our youth we aid in building this tower of rebellion.

Romans 6:16 "Know ye not, that to whom ye yield yourselves servants to obey, his servants ye are to whom ye obey; whether of sin unto death, or of obedience unto righteousness?"

James 4:4 "Ye adulterers and adulteresses, know ye not that the friendship of the world is enmity with God? whosoever, therefore, will be a friend of the world is the enemy of God."

I ONCE SERVED SATAN

I did not have to be taught how to sin; I merely had to be exposed to it. I was born with a predisposition to sin, and the more I was exposed to it, the more I embraced it. I slept with women outside of marriage without any guilt or shame, seeking only to satisfy the cravings of my flesh. I abused alcohol and drugs and enjoyed it. I flooded my mind with pornography and evil thoughts because it was entertaining and adopted the mentality of the world because it was exciting. I have lied out of selfishness to avoid the consequences of my actions and cheated because it was advantageous to me. I spent years living outside of the will of God because I thought His will dull, but through it all, it was the love of God that saved me. I made a conscious choice to no longer live for Satan and come back to the Kingdom of God.

In conclusion, whether you realized it or not, you also served Satan, and unless you made a conscious choice to return to God, you are still under his influence. When you live a life of rebellion, you are exercising your free will to live like a god, or to "Do as thou Wilt." You make your own rules and answer to no one but yourself. We live in a society where people are driven to achieve material status and success and will sacrifice everything to receive it. They will even give credit to God despite the ungodly path to achieve it as if He is responsible for their success. Not realizing Satan is the god of this world and controls its resources and riches, giving them to whomever he pleases. Note in the following verses. When Satan tempted Jesus in the wilderness, the Lord did not dispute the power, and authority Satan possessed in the earth, nor did He entertain his offer, He stood on the Word and confessed His faithfulness to God.

Luke 4:5-8
4:5 "And the devil, taking him up into an high mountain, shewed unto him all the kingdoms of the world in a moment of time."
4:6 "And the devil said unto him, All this power will I give thee, and the glory of them: for that is delivered unto me; and to whomsoever I will I give it."
4:7 "If thou, therefore, wilt worship me, all shall be thine."
4:8 "And Jesus answered and said unto him, Get thee behind me, Satan: for it is written, Thou shalt worship the Lord thy God, and him only shalt thou serve."

We worship Satan through the lives we live, and he is faithful to deliver carnal pleasures and material success to those who will live in rebellion. The more influential you are, the more he will seek to use you to carry out his agenda. Therefore, he is heavily involved in the lives of many celebrities. Knowingly, and unknowingly, they allow themselves to be exploited by him to poison the minds and hearts of their fans. He will let you believe you are "the man" and the reason behind your tremendous success. He will string you out, feed your ego, and bring pleasure and respect to your front door. Indeed, he will let you think you're in total control, assuming you can play on both sides of the fence, enjoying the world and vainly thanking God.

The truth is he will give you whatever you want, tell you whatever you want to hear, and even be your greatest cheerleader to achieve his goal - eternal possession of your soul. The result of rebellion and sin is death despite how long the process drags out. Those who trust in his twisted knowledge are left depressed, drug and alcohol addicted, paranoid, fearful, empty, broken and bound, confused and hopeless in this life. In the world to come, they will spend eternity in darkness where there is weeping and gnashing of teeth and the worm dieth not. Not to say you can't be successful and follow Christ, but the success that comes from God gives Him the glory, does not promote rebellion and sin, and involves living the truth of His Word, so others can see and receive Him.

The Power to Choose

Since the moment iniquity was found in his heart, Satan has attempted to operate outside of the design of God aspiring to be the creator as opposed to the creation. His influence has led many men down the same path, who have become vain in their imagination and allowed pride to infiltrate their hearts. Evolution suggests a design that is always changing and adapting, and The Big Bang Theory refutes the whole notion of design with the concept of random events, whereas; the Bible says the intelligent design of God created everything with a purpose and a pattern governed by Him. In other words, the Bible lets us know God is always in control, and we must operate in the framework He created as opposed to being stubborn and rebellious.

Romans 1:20-21
1:20 "For the invisible things of him from the creation of the world are clearly seen, being understood by the things that are made, [even] his eternal power and Godhead; so that they are without excuse:
1:21 "Because that, when they knew God, they glorified [him] not as God, neither were thankful; but became

vain in their imaginations, and their foolish heart was darkened.

1:22 "Professing themselves to be wise, they became fools,"

Sin is the act of operating outside of the design of God and refusing to submit to His instructions. At its core, it is not always a matter of good and evil, but obedience versus rebellion. Let's consider the forbidden tree in the Garden of Eden. The Bible says the tree was good for food, pleasant to the eyes, and a tree to be desired to make one wise meaning there was nothing inherently wrong with the tree. The issue was Adam's disobedience to God's instructions.

What some people fail to realize when discussing the forbidden tree is Adam and Eve had every other tree in the garden to choose. The Bible goes on to say the other trees were also pleasant to the sight and good for food the same as the forbidden tree. Temptation is not based on neglect; rather; what you can't have. The choices Adam and Eve had far exceeded the one they did not. In our own lives' temptation derives from a lack of contentment and appreciation for the framework God created. Since the beginning of time, Satan has used the same three tactics to draw men into sin and rebellion. Within every sin and temptation, you will find one or more of these spirits operating: The lust of the Eyes, The Lust of the Flesh, and The Pride of Life. Consider how prevalent these satanic spirits are in society today.

The Bible contains God's blueprint built on trust, faith, and obedience. We are called to trust in His design, have faith in His plan and purpose, and to be obedient to His instructions. Choosing to do so is exercising our love and commitment to Him while reverencing Him as our creator. The nature of sin is self-governance, self-will, self-gratification, and a desire to ascend above the authority of God. Sin breeds justification, which is the process of reasoning away the commandments of God and replacing His instructions with our ideas of good and evil. These ideas are drawn from societal norms of acceptable and unacceptable behavior that change over time.

For example, look at the issue of same-sex marriage. The Bible says marriage is between a man and a woman in agreement with the sovereign design of

God. Increasingly, the societal view states there is no harm in two committed people who love each other getting married even if they happen to be the same sex. The argument is if the couple is in love, cares for each other, and makes each other happy then shouldn't they be afforded the same rights to marriage as a heterosexual couple?

The more these points considered, the more pressure to challenge the design of God even though we live in a country which in the past chose to adopt the Biblical definition of marriage. The argument becomes if God is love and two people loving each other is a good thing, why would a loving God be opposed to the happiness of two committed people? The same type of reasoning Eve may have used while looking at the tree the Bible says was good. The result of logic and rationalizing the instructions of God, as opposed to accepting those instructions, is a series of choices.

Given the fact we are born with a revelation of the existence of God, it is natural to seek some sort of spiritual validation for our behavior. Otherwise, people must find the courage to admit they don't choose to believe the Bible. Either we must declare the Bible is full of loopholes and claim it is nothing more than a reference point and should not be taken literally. View it as a book of non-binding suggestions and maintain it is man's opinion and not the will of God. Make the argument the times have changed, and God just forgot to update the book, or abandon the book altogether and discredit those people who still choose to believe in it. The latter option has always been Satan's plan, but he knew he couldn't snatch the Bible out of our hands. Instead, it had to be gently massaged and deliberately loosed from our grip. Ten years ago, who would have dreamed of seeing a day in which the Bible is discredited, attacked, mocked, and blatantly misinterpreted the way it is today, or Christians viewed as hateful, insensitive, and intolerant of others to discredit them and drive them from all circles of influence? Or better yet, someone would lose their job for merely supporting marriage between a man and a woman? No matter how hard they attempt to twist, bend, and manipulate the words, the Bible does not change, and it will continue to stand in the way of those who refuse to heed to its instructions.

For most Christians, the marriage debate is not a matter of hate and discrimination but a choice to accept the Biblical definition of marriage. To accuse someone of hatred or intolerance because he chooses to believe the Bible is the persecution the bible warned would come as a result of standing on the truth. Do you see other religions attacked that hold the same views on marriage? Do I hate the fornicator or whoremonger because I advocate for abstinence outside of marriage? Do I hate the drug user or alcoholic because I defend the power of Christ to set them free, or the liar and deceiver because I stand for truth? Did my mother hate me, or was she sexophobic every time she told me I shouldn't be living with a woman who was not my wife? Would Adam have hated Eve if he had told her not to bite the forbidden fruit? Of course not, it is merely advocating the design and plan of God according to the Bible in love. The choice is left to the individual what he/she chooses to believe and should never be the result of force, coercion, or hateful behavior. We are all free to choose as we wish, but we are also free to believe what we choose. We are all born with something we must surrender to God, and it is through preaching God speaks to His people. We have all lived outside of the will of God and taken a bite of the forbidden fruit, and many of us have eaten the leaves and tree bark as well. I advocate the love of God and the power of the Cross to deliver us from anything preventing us from living in His design.

Before surrendering my life to Christ, it was never my perception the many people who shared the Bible with me along the way hated me because they didn't agree with the way I lived. I just thought they were Christians and it was my choice at the time to live my life outside of the Bible. I knew what the Bible taught, and it came as no surprise they didn't agree with the way I was living my life. I even argued with some, challenged others, but deep down I knew they were only reading the book, and there came a time in my life when I discovered my argument was not with them but with the Bible. I found there were a lot of things I could be in life, but if I were going to be a Christian, then I would have to follow Christ. The Bible has been around for centuries, so it should not come as a surprise or shock, especially in America, what Christians believe. Our beliefs have not changed because the Bible has not changed, but society has changed, and the friction exists because we refuse to change with it. The day soon approaches when the mask will come off, the real agenda made known, and the true enemy of the world revealed which is the Bible.

Christianity does not preach hate but revelation. Everyone has a choice. At no time will you ever see me picketing outside of someone's bedroom, but always I will exercise my right to believe the Bible and to live my life accordingly. I, too, had to decide whether I was going to accept the Bible. I finally came to the realization God wasn't going to change the Bible to accommodate my lifestyle, so I had to change my lifestyle to accommodate God.

The following excerpt from my book **"<u>Why God Kept Saving M</u>e"** is a snapshot of how I once rejected the truth.

"I began to feel more at ease as they watered down my religion to a place more comfortable, assuring me I was still a Christian. Instead of learning to be like Jesus, which I was beginning to feel was out of my reach; I started to see a God that would accept me in whatever state He found me. If this were my lifestyle, then God would approve if I acknowledged Him. I began to convince myself God did not pay much attention to us individually to monitor our every move. I started to believe in collective responsibility, and if I were going the speed of traffic, then I would not be pulled over despite the fact I was exceeding the speed limit.

I listened as they justified themselves by discussing the Bible to assure me, they were as saved as the next person. "I have a good relationship with God," they would say. They pointed out how Jesus had turned the water to "wine." Therefore; drinking was nothing new. The key was not to get drunk. Drunk to them was completely blacking out, and anything short of that was fine. The book of Ecclesiastic tells us "to drink and be merry," another argued. The more scripture they gave me, the better I felt about my condition. It didn't matter that there were tons of other scriptures we violated if we could justify our lifestyle choices. It was always something we were doing to make the lifestyle bad rather than the lifestyle itself."

"I sank even further as I ate every word the slurring prophets fed me. It was easier to believe the deception than face my failure. I didn't fail; I just went overboard. Not to believe them meant I was an utter failure and I would be forced to accept the fact I just refused to surrender my life to God. How does one swallow that pill? To openly admit I wasn't ready to surrender my life to God was to tell God I enjoyed my lifestyle at the expense of not having Him in it. That I was willing to gamble on going to hell to enjoy the things I was not ready to give up. Even though God knew my heart, I could never acknowledge such an idiotic decision, so I had no choice but to believe the deception. They were telling me what I wanted to hear, much the same as I had told them on previous occasions. I had played this game of justifying my behavior so many times in the past. Now, some of the things they told me were the very things I had used on them. I knew deep down I had accepted a lie, but the more I embraced that lie, the more it became my truth. My friends only enhanced the evil workings of my mind. God wouldn't send all of us to hell, I reasoned. Maybe He does understand. I mean, look at all the people who were doing the same things we were. Everywhere I went, people were dominated by thoughts of partying, sex, and having a good time. You could go all day without hearing God's name mentioned. Most people I encountered in life were holding a drink in their hand or scheming on the opposite sex. Those who did talk about religion were at the very least, fornicating. It seemed as if their faith was based on success and if they appeared to be moving forward in life, certain sins were acceptable. There were a few people I knew that were for real, but they did not frequent the same places I did, so I hardly ever saw them.

As fate would have it, most of the people I came across were very new in the faith without a solid foundation, so I even challenged their beliefs. I attacked their weaknesses as they attempted to share the Word with me by turning the questions back on them. I would ask them if they were perfect. When they answered "No," I would question how they could say they were any closer to God than I was. I was quick to tell them they were sinning every time they judged my lifestyle. The scriptures put up no fight as I merely forced them into place to fit my distorted puzzle. I was not seeking the truth anymore; I only sought to justify myself by ignoring any scriptures that spoke against my lifestyle. I had no conception of mercy and grace, and in my ignorance, I thought I could somehow legitimize my actions. I even started to believe I was convincing God. Even when the truth was right in front of my face, it had no impact on me because I had become such a master at ignoring it. My truths were so unstable they would change from day to day depending on what sounded good to me."

Why God Kept Saving Me

<u>Prayer</u>

God the Father, Eternal God and Father of Lights. Lord
of Host who is not a million miles away, but right here
with us each day, able to hear our petitions and willing
to help us in our time of need. Just and Righteous God
whose word is sure and commandments are not
grievous. In the name of your Only Begotten Son, Jesus
Christ, Spirit of Wisdom and Understanding, we come
before your great and holy throne declaring our undying
faith in your word. We stand on your sure and precious
promises, knowing you place your word above your
name. It will not return unto you void, but accomplish
all you please, and prosper in the thing where you sent
it. In the name of Jesus and the power of His Blood, we
ask, Lord, that you will have compassion on us,
according to your loving kindness and the multitude of
thy tender mercies. We stand before your throne, Lord,
naked before the truth and guilty as charged. We
acknowledge our transgressions before you, and our sin
is not hidden from your sight for we were shaped in
iniquity and in sin were we conceived. In the name of

97

Jesus and the power of His Blood, we acknowledge our shortcomings and weaknesses and confess any sin in our lives, both known and unknown. We humble ourselves and ask you to examine the hidden places of our hearts and the most remote areas of our minds, holding back nothing and revealing all things to you. In the name of Jesus, we ask you to examine our motives and the intentions of our heart and let us live righteously in your sight. Grant us a heart to turn away from all rebellion and anything not lined up with your will and help us to be easily convicted and quick to get things right with you. For you are the Creator and we are clay in your hands. In the name of Jesus, we trust you, Heavenly Father, to cleanse us from all unrighteousness and establish us firmly in the truth. In Jesus name, we pray. Thank God. Amen.

The Absolute Case for Jesus Christ

Romans 5:12 "Wherefore, as by one man sin entered into the world, and death by sin; and so death passed upon all men, for that all have sinned:"

From the moment Adam disobeyed God in the Garden of Eden, every man born from his seed inherited a fallen nature which is inherently evil and rooted in sin and rebellion. We do not all battle the same thing but make no mistake about it; we are all born in darkness battling our fallen nature. The fallen nature seeks independence from the design of God, as opposed to submission and obedience to His will. The result is physical and spiritual death, which is eternal separation from God.

Romans 6:23 "For the wages of sin is death; but the gift of God is eternal life through Jesus Christ our Lord."

When discussing accepting or changing man's nature, the argument is made "I was born this way." Proponents of this thought believe who we are is a matter of birth and not choice, therefore; God must have designed us to be this way or He loves us the way we are. They believe man is born inherently good. Therefore, change is not possible, nor is it necessary. The truth is no one chooses his make up at birth, and the Bible clearly states **we were not created the way we are born**. How God created man and our birth into this world are two separate matters. So, when people say "take it up with my creator," the Bible already has.

As stated in the previous chapter, The Fall of Man, it is critical to understand God's original design for man was altered as a result of Adam's disobedience resulting in all men being born into sin and in need of salvation. In other words, the choice made for us, and we are all born into this world needing deliverance and a Savior. The choice God has given us is whether we will surrender our fallen nature to Him. The love of God based on choice, not acceptance, and we are not innocent until proven guilty when it comes to our fallen nature. We are born into this world guilty and in need of an advocate.

Romans 3:23 "For all have sinned, and come short of the glory of God;"

The great news is we have an advocate and a
way to escape our fallen nature because salvation and
deliverance were made possible through the Lord Jesus
Christ.

Romans 5:19
5:19 "For as by one man's disobedience many were
made sinners, so by the obedience of one shall many be
made righteous."

He was obedient unto death, and His sacrifice in dying
on the cross guaranteed all that would receive Him a
way to overcome his fallen nature.

God's plan of redemption for man is the full
expression of His love and began before man even fell.
Before the world formed, God made way for man to be
redeemed.

Ephesians 1:3-5
1:3 "Blessed *be* the God and Father of our Lord Jesus
Christ, who hath blessed us with all spiritual blessings
in heavenly *places* in Christ:"
1:4 "According as he hath chosen us in him before the
foundation of the world, that we should be holy and
without blame before him in love:"
1:5 "Having predestinated us unto the adoption of
children by Jesus Christ to himself, according to the
good pleasure of his will,"
1:6 "To the praise of the glory of his grace, wherein he
hath made us accepted in the beloved."

1:7 "In whom we have redemption through his blood, the forgiveness of sins, according to the riches of his grace;"

Jesus Christ was the very best God could give. Because He is holy, and in Him is no sin at all. Only He could die on the cross for our sins. Redemption was not earned or deserved, nor was it the inherent right of man to be redeemed. It was granted solely at the discretion of God who knew the price of sin was eternal separation from Him. Consistent with His original design, His plan was based on man's choice to receive His gift. God desires a family that will choose to love Him as opposed to being forced to love Him.

Our fate was not sealed that unfortunate day in the Garden of Eden when Adam disobeyed God. Once again, Satan had been successful in leading God's creation astray, but he drastically underestimated His love for man. We were given an opportunity to return to Him. While trapped in sin with no answer or hope, wholly lost in a state of rebellion and rejection, God performed the ultimate act of love. He gave the most precious and dearest gift He had. Perhaps the one gift the God of all creation only had one of, His only

Begotten Son, Jesus Christ, the perfect sacrifice to atone for our sins. He was perfect in all ways, but out of God's great love for man, He willingly offered His Son to shed His innocent blood on behalf of our sins.

John 3:16 "For God so loved the world, that he gave his only begotten Son, that whosoever believeth in him should not perish, but have everlasting life."

Romans 5:6-9
5:6 "For when we were yet without strength, in due time Christ died for the ungodly."
5:7 "For scarcely for a righteous man will one die: yet peradventure for a good man some would even dare to die."
5:8 "But God commendeth his love toward us, in that, while we were yet sinners, Christ died for us."
5:9 "Much more then, being now justified by his blood, we shall be saved from wrath through him."

I remember a time in our nation when making a case for Jesus Christ would have been preaching to the choir, but as the day draws near for Christ's return, Satan has intensified his efforts against the church and the person of Jesus Christ. He is a great deceiver, full of wisdom and extremely calculating, and has already caused countless souls to fall victim to his shrewd influence. Satan doesn't care if you're religious, sing in

103

the choir, or built a church with your bare hands; He plans to destroy the role of Jesus Christ by making Him irrelevant to salvation.

I say with confidence, and every fiber of my being there is no more significant statement in Christianity than the absolute importance of Jesus Christ, who He was, who He is, and the work accomplished through His death, His burial, and resurrection.

Romans 1:16 "For I am not ashamed of the gospel of Christ: for it is the power of God unto salvation to every one that believeth; to the Jew first, and also to the Greek."

Without an absolute and unwavering belief in Jesus Christ, Christianity is nothing more than a pagan exercise.

Who He was: Before Jesus Christ manifested in the form of a man, He was the living Word, and in the book of Revelation He is once again referred to as the Word when He makes His glorious return. He is the very expression of God, His thoughts, His will, His design, and plan for all creation. He was and continues to be both with God and God. He was with God from the beginning, and all things were made by Him and through Him, and He will remain with Him through eternity.

John 1:1-3; 14
1:1 "In the beginning was the Word, and the Word was with God, and the Word was God."
1:2 "The same was in the beginning with God."
1:3 "All things were made by him; and without him was not any thing made that was made."
1:14 "And the Word was made flesh, and dwelt among us, (and we beheld his glory, the glory as of the only begotten of the Father,) full of grace and truth."

Matthew 1:18-20
1:18 "Now the birth of Jesus Christ was on this wise: When as his mother Mary was espoused to Joseph, before they came together, she was found with child of the Holy Ghost."
1:19 "Then Joseph her husband, being a just man, and not willing to make her a publick example, was minded to put her away privily."
1:20 "But while he thought on these things, behold, the angel of the Lord appeared unto him in a dream, saying, Joseph, thou son of David, fear not to take unto thee Mary thy wife: for that which is conceived in her is of the Holy Ghost."
1:21 "And she shall bring forth a son, and thou shalt call his name JESUS: for he shall save his people from their sins."
1:22 "Now all this was done, that it might be fulfilled which was spoken of the Lord by the prophet, saying,"

1:23 "Behold, a virgin shall be with child, and shall bring forth a son, and they shall call his name Emmanuel, which being interpreted is, God with us."

John 10:30 "I and my Father are one."

Revelation 19:13 "And he was clothed with a vesture dipped in blood: and his name is called The Word of God."

He was born of a virgin in the flesh (John 1:14) to redeem mankind from his fall being He was the only perfect sacrifice acceptable to God to make atonement for our sins. He was not born through the seed of a man, so He was untainted by Adam's corruptible seed having no sin, spot, or blemish. In other words, every descendant of Adam inherits Adam's DNA (fallen nature). To redeem man, the sacrifice had to be perfect and pure, coming from a different bloodline. Jesus was not born the descendant of man, but rather the descendant of God. His blood was pure and untainted. To be born again is to die to Adam's DNA and to be reborn with the DNA of Christ.

He shed His innocent blood on the cross paying the ultimate price for our sins. Being unjustly taken to the pit of Hell, He destroyed the curse of sin and death, which had us bound and defeated by Satan who exercised authority over the fallen nature of man. The grave proved powerless to hold Him, and on the third day, He was resurrected having finished the redemptive plan of God. He rose with all power and authority, crushing principalities and powers of darkness and stripping Satan of his authority over God's children who would choose to be redeemed. Jesus Christ, being obedient unto death, was everything God needed Him to be, and the hope we have as Christians is **who He was, He continues to be.**

Colossians 1:12-14
1:12 "Giving thanks unto the Father, which hath made us meet to be partakers of the inheritance of the saints in light:"
1:13 "Who hath delivered us from the power of darkness, and hath translated us into the kingdom of his dear Son:"
1:14 "In whom we have redemption through his blood, even the forgiveness of sins:"

Philippians 2:8-11
2:8 "And being found in fashion as a man, he humbled himself, and became obedient unto death, even the death of the cross."
2:9 "Wherefore God also hath highly exalted him, and given him a name which is above every name:"

107

2:10 "That at the name of Jesus every knee should bow, of things in heaven, and things in earth, and things under the earth;"
2:11 "And that every tongue should confess that Jesus Christ is Lord, to the glory of God the Father."

I. John 3:8 "He that committeth sin is of the devil; for the devil sinneth from the beginning. For this purpose the Son of God was manifested, that he might destroy the works of the devil."

Who He is: He is the mediator between God and man.

Romans 5:9 states we are justified by His blood shed

for us on the cross, and through Him and Him alone, we

have peace with God. He is our Savior who redeemed

us from the fall.

II Corinthians 5:21
5:21 "For he hath made him to be sin for us, who knew no sin; that we might be made the righteousness of God in him."

We are given assurance in the book of Romans He is

the embodiment of God's covenant with man.

Romans 10:13 "For whosoever shall call upon the name of the Lord shall be saved."

He is our appointed advocate who confesses our names

before the Father and makes intercession on our behalf.

He is our comforter who gives us consolation and peace through every trial and storm, our way maker who leads us in the paths of righteousness for His name's sake, and our friend who sticks closer than a brother. He is our protector who walks with us through the valley of the shadow of death, shielding us from every weapon of Satan. He is our counselor who directs our thoughts, our healer who cures our sickness and infirmities, and our source of life and strength. In Him we have hope for eternal life being He was more than just a good man that walked the earth performing miracles, casting out devils, healing the sick, and dying for a just cause. His accomplishments extend far past the limitations of the grave and the confines of death in which mere men would be bound. His work on the cross completed the plan of God, opened the door for renewal and transformation, reversed every curse of sickness, poverty and death and all other consequences stemming from the fall, and He granted universal access for all men to the very throne of God. Certain without a doubt, Jesus Christ is the breath and heartbeat of Christianity, and its sole purpose for existence is to introduce the world to Him.

Jesus is the Only Way:

John 14:6 "Jesus saith unto him, I am the way, the truth, and the life: no man cometh unto the Father, but by me."

Matthew 10:32-33
10:32 "Whosoever therefore shall confess me before men, him will I confess also before my Father which is in heaven."
10:33 "But whosoever shall deny me before men, him will I also deny before my Father which is in heaven."

II. Timothy 2:12-13
2:12 "If we suffer, we shall also reign with [him]: if we deny [him], he also will deny us:"
2:13 "If we believe not, [yet] he abideth faithful: he cannot deny himself."

I. John 5:12 "He that hath the Son hath life; [and] he that hath not the Son of God hath not life."

Through Him, we are called to preach the unadulterated word of God. We can no longer be vague and confusing when it comes to the question of Jesus Christ. The foundation of Christianity rests on the revelation Jesus Christ is the Messiah, the Son of the living God. As Christians, our faith is predicated on the belief He is the way, the truth, and the life, and no man cometh unto the Father but by Him. An issue which speaks to the very foundation of what we profess to believe as Christians. As believers of Jesus Christ, we must be ready to take a stand without wavering to represent His interest even in the face of the mounting pressures to be politically correct. "He is the only way to salvation," meaning there is no other way and leaves no room to waiver if you genuinely believe what you confess. To confess Jesus Christ before men, you must be willing to stand witness for Him in the face of all doubt, persecution, and disbelief. Our hope is others may also believe in Him through our words.

The process of dying to our old nature to be like Christ involves chastisement and correction, which is not consistent with politically correct thought.

Hebrews 12:6-8; 11
6:6 "For whom the Lord loveth he chasteneth, and scourgeth every son whom he receiveth."
6:7 "If ye endure chastening, God dealeth with you as with sons; for what son is he whom the father chasteneth not?
6:8 "But if ye be without chastisement, whereof all are partakers, then are ye bastards, and not sons."

111

6:11 "Now no chastening for the present seemeth to be joyous, but grievous: nevertheless afterward it yieldeth the peaceable fruit of righteousness unto them which are exercised thereby."

The Bible is designed to convict man of his sin, stir the consciousness, and prick the heart to turn him away from his fallen nature which must be redeemed, and not accommodated. This is accomplished by receiving revelation from the Bible and then deciding to turn away from those ways not lined up with His Word. This idea, according to political correctness, is offensive, hateful, hurtful, insensitive, and harmful to the environment. Not to mention the high treason committed by uttering, there is a place called hell where people go if they remain in a fallen state.

The aim of Christianity is not reaching a consensus, conforming to the world, universalism, or finding common ground. It's about being a disciple of the Lord Jesus Christ. It is a decision to follow the examples of Christ in the face of persecution, to think differently in the light of the negative labels and slander you may endure, and not being afraid to take a stand in the minority even if it seems as if the whole world is standing against you. You will often have to abstain when others are eager to participate, to speak out when your words may cause you to be ostracized, and to believe the Bible when it is the unpopular thing to do.

The Bible says we are encamped about by a great cloud of witnesses. Men and women mocked for what they believed, imprisoned for no cause, tortured for amusement, and stoned and beaten to death. Not to mention Jesus Christ, who endured unimaginable pain and suffering on our behalf and paid the ultimate price of death for our freedom. It is a disservice to these brave men and women of God when we waiver on the question of Jesus Christ in the face of mere embarrassment, the fear of offending someone, or unjustly being labeled as an insensitive hate monger.

These men and women did not base their beliefs on the approval of the crowd and remained faithful to Him. They understood our beliefs are not validated by opinion polls, media influence, the mood of the masses, or celebrity approval. They are inspired by the Bible from the very breathe of God. The truth is the world doesn't have a problem with religion as evidenced by

113

the creation of a world religious organization and the rise of ecumenism. The world has a problem with Jesus Christ and the people who boldly proclaim He is the only way. We must be cognizant of the world's agenda to replace Jesus Christ with the concept of religion, rendering Him irrelevant and nothing more than a good man.

<u>Prayer</u>

In the name of Jesus, The Author and the Finisher of
our faith. The Beloved Son of the Most High God, The
Prince of Peace and Lord of Lords, we humbly come
before your throne, Heavenly Father. We come in the
knowledge and revelation of the truth in Christ Jesus,
our Lord. He is the Way, the Truth, and the Life, and no
man can come unto the Father but by Him. In the name
of Jesus, we walk into the light and company of Angels
who live and profess the same, kneeling before your
throne and giving praise to your name. In the name of
Jesus and the power of His Blood, we answer the
Universal Call sent out to all men inviting your children
to come back into fellowship with you, for you are no
respecter of persons and all men are entitled to receive
your gift. Any man who thirsts for the Bread of Life
will be filled with rivers of living water. Your word
says everyone who calls on the name of the Lord shall
be saved and not perish but inherit the gift of Eternal
Life.

We stand before you, Lord, guilty as charged, born into sin and in desperate need of a Savior and hope. We acknowledge our sins and fallen nature and the rebellion that sits at the door of our hearts and choose His Precious Blood to wash away all iniquity. We die to this old nature riddled with the imperfections of men and choose to be born again through the life, burial, and resurrection of Christ. In the name of Jesus, we exercise choice and free will you have given us to declare before the Heavens and the earth that Jesus is indeed the Christ, the Son of the Living God. We choose His Blood to cover our sins and repent of all unrighteousness. Our choice is you, Lord, and we inherit all rights and responsibilities, your statutes and commandments, and the choice to surrender our will for your own. We die to all carnal thoughts and worldliness being refreshed and renewed in the knowledge of Christ. We answer the Universal Call to turn away from all rebellion and confess we are saved and covered by His precious Blood. In Jesus name, we pray. Thank God – Amen.

A Universal Call

The gift of salvation is contingent on man accepting the offer according to the terms set forth by God, so it is a gift with strings attached. Giving His Only Begotten Son was a unilateral act performed when man was in his worst state and total disobedience to His will. He did it for all men and extended the offer to all that would receive Him. Refusing to accept Jesus Christ is a conscious choice not to receive the gift. Heaven and Hell is not a matter of God's love, as some would have you to believe, for God so loved the world He gave His only Begotten Son.

God is love in the purest form. It has always been a matter of man choosing to accept the design and plan of God. If you choose to reject God's offer, it is not the love of God that causes eternal separation, but your choice. Once again, the fallen nature of man must be redeemed, and redemption is a matter of choice. You are born into this world in rebellion, and you are free to stay that way if that is your choice.

The choice is made available to all men, and anyone can decide to receive Jesus Christ as their Lord and Savior regardless of their past, lifestyle, culture, gender, race, or any other characteristic. By faith, we bring all our shortcomings, weaknesses, and sin to Him abandoning our old nature and being born again in His. In other words, we can't hide behind the excuse "I was born this way" and must be willing to trust Him and His word to deliver us from the fallen nature we were born. The whole purpose of salvation is to deliver us from the fall, not to merely cover it up and pretend it never happened. There is no sacrifice man can give that compares to the blood shed by Jesus Christ

Have you exercised your choice to accept Jesus Christ into your life? Did you once receive Jesus Christ as your Lord and savior but have since fallen away? Are you looking to be more committed to Him and obedient to His word? If you answered yes to any of these questions, now is your time to make it right with God. In this very moment, God is speaking to your heart and reading this book is no coincidence. Ask Jesus Christ into your life and receive Him as your personal Lord and savior. The Bible tells us we must believe in our heart He is the only Begotten Son of God. He died on the Cross for our sins, and He rose again from the grave. If you are willing to confess the same with your mouth, you can receive salvation right now. Speak to Him from the depths of your heart. Ask Him to forgive you for your sins, and then accept the gift of salvation He offers through His son Jesus Christ. You are not alone, and each of us that have received Him came down this same path. It doesn't matter what you have been struggling with, how long you have lived outside of His will, or how egregious your disobedience has been, He will receive you and will not turn you away.

John 6:37 "All that the Father giveth me shall come to me; and him that cometh to me I will in no wise cast out."

I have included an excerpt from my book **"Why God Kept Saving Me,"** which is my testimony of how I accepted the gift of salvation. As much as I wanted to change my life, as obvious as the signs of deterioration may have been, and regardless how many people told me there was a better way, I was bound to the nature I was born. There were even times where I, too, hid behind the excuse "I was born this way," and saw no way of escape. My sinful nature had become so familiar to me I began to embrace it which led me to justify my choices and behavior because I felt I had no other option but to accept it to find some sense of peace. I was indeed a slave to the influences which surrounded me and the limitations of the feelings and emotions that shaped my consciousness. Then I had an encounter with Him, and it changed my life forever. I make an absolute case for the Lord Jesus Christ and His ability to deliver us from whatever we are battling with if we first decide to trust in Him.

Excerpt from the book "Why God Kept Saving Me"

I bent over as I felt sharp pains run through my stomach. I slowly walked over to a mirror and looked at myself. I was so afraid of what I saw staring back at me and could not believe what I had become. I began to cry uncontrollably as I thought about my wife and how she was the closest thing to purity in my life. I felt like a coward as if I had shot her in the back. I could not bear the thought of having betrayed her. I thought about losing everything the Lord had given me, including my soul. The idea of not having God in my life drove me crazy, and I began to cry even harder. My relationship with God, my wife, everything I had in life was about to be lost. It did not matter how good the apple looked or how tasty it may have been; the result was there was always a worm in the middle. I sat in the room for hours, crying myself to sleep, waking up, and then crying myself back to sleep. I even considered going to get something to drink and then drink myself into unconsciousness. The thought of completely giving up seemed to be my only option.

The more I thought about it, the more another voice told me that if I took that drink, I would die. I felt I was at the final crossroad in my life facing one last choice. I knew beyond a doubt if I jumped in my truck and drove off into the streets, I wasn't coming back. It was as if the Devil was waiting on me so he could make his final assault on my life. I was feeling so bad and empty each time the thought came to my mind. I grabbed my keys and headed towards the front door. Even though I knew I was not coming back, I took precious moments contemplating leaving. I felt the Devil had beaten me, and I had no other choice but to obey him and surrender. As much as the Devil hated me, I thought I deserved to be hated. The more I pondered over the choice, the stronger the other voice got and continued to say, "Do not go!"

As confused and exhausted as I was, I decided I needed to have one last talk with God. I was entirely out of options in life. I could not turn to the left or the right. I could not go forward or backward, and I could not look up or down. I could not rely on people, not even talk to my wife. There was not a person in the world that could give me what I desperately needed. I went home and went into a closet to pray. I sat down on the floor, opened my mouth and I began to speak.

I went into the closet prepared not ever to come back out. I had never before experienced the soundness in my mind I had at that moment. I had never been so sincere before in my life, and I made a single request to God. I knew God was real and would hear my prayer. I knew He loved me because He had shown me so many times before. I also knew God wasn't the problem; I was the problem. He had rescued me so many times before so I was convinced, He would answer my prayer. I asked God the best way I knew to either change me that instant or bring me up right then and there. I told Him I was fully prepared to take my last breath in that closet if I could not come out a changed man. Deep down, I loved God, and I did not want to go to hell. I knew if I left that closet the same way I came in hell would be my home.

It was more than just the agony of being in hell; it was the painful thought of being separated from God. Painful as it would have been to lose everything I had in life, the idea of losing God was the one thing I could not bear. The most horrible thought I ever had was opening my eyes in hell. How could anyone face the reality of being eternally separated from God?

Tears began streaming down my face as I repeatedly apologized to God, not just for what happened earlier that day, but for everything. I had come to the very end of myself and was entirely out of compromises and schemes to live the way I wanted to or beat the Devil. I told God I was never going to come up with a way to live on both sides of the fence, and I needed Him to take complete control over my life.

I came to terms with the fact I was the one that continued to hold on to my old lifestyle. Whatever your will is God is what I will do. Whatever you want me to give up, whoever I have to stop hanging with, places I have to stop going, whatever God, and I won't offer any resistance anymore. I told God I wanted Him to be first and foremost in my life, and I would surrender all to Him. Suddenly, friends did not seem so important anymore, and hanging out and partying was the farthest things from my mind. Please, God, either take me up to be with you while I'm in this closet or change me because I cannot leave this closet the same way I came in. I found myself reciting the most sincere words I had ever spoken. I was finally convinced I had to quit relying on myself and rely on God. This was an all or nothing decision. I could not live with one foot in the Church and one foot in the world. As I continued to pray, I felt a tingling sensation began to travel up my body, first at my feet. The feeling proceeded to travel up my leg on through my stomach and up my chest.

The sensation went up through my head; I felt a tremendous burden lifted off of me. I felt something heavy being pulled off of my shoulders. It was a very peaceful and comforting feeling as if all the heaviness I had ever experienced in life stripped from me. It was as if I was opening my eyes for the very first time. My tears were instantly dried up. The painful emptiness I had felt for so many years was no longer there.

I knew in that instant I was forgiven. God told me I was forgiven and I believed Him. Even though I knew I did not deserve forgiveness, God told me to accept His gift. I knew I would never be the same again! The Lord told me He would turn my sorrow to rejoicing and share His love with me. I forgot about all the pain and sorrow I had come into the closet with, and I felt refreshed and rejuvenated. This feeling was unlike anything I had ever felt before because I knew I was delivered. I had been crucified with Christ and born again. I did not even feel the same. I felt like a new man that had been set free. I could visualize my shackles broken and the prison doors bursting open. I

experienced the undisputed, unquestionable, changing
power of Jesus Christ, the Son of God.

But who do you say I the Son of man am?

Matthew 16:13-18
16:13 "When Jesus came into the coasts of Caesarea
Philippi, he asked his disciples, saying, Whom do men
say that I the Son of man am?"
16:14 "And they said, Some *say that thou art* John the
Baptist: some, Elias; and others, Jeremias, or one of the
prophets."
16:15 "He saith unto them, But whom say ye that I
am?"
16:16 "And Simon Peter answered and said, Thou art
the Christ, the Son of the living God."
16:17 "And Jesus answered and said unto him, Blessed
art thou, Simon Barjona: for flesh and blood hath not
revealed *it* unto thee, but my Father which is in
heaven."
16:18 "And I say also unto thee, That thou art Peter,
and upon this rock I will build my church; and the gates
of hell shall not prevail against it."

When Jesus asked the question "Whom say ye
that I am?", Peter boldly replied, "You are the
Messiah, the Son of the living God." You see, Jesus
was a lot of things to a lot of people. Some thought he
was just another prophet, some felt he was a great man,
to others he was a healer, but Peter had received a

126

revelation from God He was the Christ and God's Only Begotten Son.

It is upon divinely inspired truth the gospel stands and it upon truth men are delivered and born again. Each one of us must answer the same question **"Who is Jesus going to be in your life**?" Is He just a man who can neither save nor deliver or the Messiah? As a Christian, you must be willing to bet everything on this revelation. You must be willing to boldly proclaim to the world Jesus Christ is the Son of the Living God, and He is the head of your life. It is upon this solid truth the Lord said He would build His church. It is upon this revelation we have eternal life. It is upon this revelation we enter a covenant with God, and it is upon this revelation we inherit His supernatural DNA. It is upon this revelation we no longer have to say, **"I was born this way,"** believing He was more than just a man and capable of delivering us from anything that has us bound or operating outside of the design and plan and God. It is upon this revelation we endure all heartache and pain and the persecution that will follow. It is upon this revelation we remain faithful until death and are willing to suffer ridicule and embarrassment on His behalf. It is upon this revelation we do not back down when asked Is He the only way or what our stance is on issues such as marriage and abortion, or the neglect of the poor. It upon this revelation, we are willing to repent and trust His Word for deliverance. It is our blessed hope in which we have confidence He will love us, provide for us, and teach us how to be like Him. It is a sober thought laced with sorrows, setbacks, sacrifices, disappointments, and pain, but a price worth paying for the eternal and victorious life we inherit through Him.

John 14:6 "Jesus saith unto him, I am the way, the truth, and the life: no man cometh unto the Father, but by me."

You are not waiting on God; God is waiting on you. Waiting for the day and moment, you will look to Him to be delivered from your old nature and not merely rescued from your bad decisions. The day when you will recognize Jesus Christ is the very Son of God and Creator of all things. That day when you have come to the end of yourself and realize you must be willing to surrender all to Him. The day you set aside your arrogance and pride and humbly recognize He is the only hope you have in this world and one day you will

stand before Him and give an account of your life.

Isaiah 59:1-2
59:1 "Behold, the LORD'S hand is not shortened, that it
cannot save; neither his ear heavy, that it cannot hear:"
59:2 "But your iniquities have separated between you
and your God, and your sins have hid *his* face from
you, that he will not hear."

Romans 14:11-12
14:11 "For it is written, *As* I live, saith the Lord, every
knee shall bow to me, and every tongue shall confess to
God."
14:12 "So then every one of us shall give account of
himself to God."

Prayer

Praises be to the Most High God. The God of Abraham, Isaac, and Jacob, the Holy One of Israel, the Alpha and the Omega, the Beginning and the End. From everlasting to everlasting, the Only Wise God. God of great mercy and grace whose covenants span eternity and whose word is sure. Living God, who is the judge of all things and whose compassion is a fortress surrounding the hearts of His people. Your faithfulness is our hope, and we rest in your promises. We come before your throne in the name of our Lord and Savior Jesus Christ, the unspotted and unblemished Lamb of the sovereign God. The Lion of the Tribe of Judah and Heir of all things. The Lord of righteousness and Most Holy Prince of Life. In the Spirit of grace and mercy, we humbly approach your throne. We come in the hope of your word and the finished work of the Cross and pray we are found worthy to be named in the Lambs Book of Life. Not by works in which we have done, but by the shedding of His Blood and the gift of redemption we have received in His name. For your word says He was wounded for our rebellion, bruised for our sin, and the punishment that brought us peace was upon Him, but in His suffering, we were made whole. In His precious name, the name of Jesus Christ, we thank you for the great price paid on our behalf.

We thank you, Dear Father, for the significance of the Blood and its ability to revive, replenish, refresh and restore. It brings nourishment and life to the body while eliminating every detrimental and harmful thing. His Blood signifies our high birth into your royal lineage and through the Blood, your characteristics are ingrained in our DNA. Though we were men dead in trespasses and sin, His Blood removes all impurities from our minds and hearts, and we are no longer bound by a sin consciousness. We are free to walk in the newness of life, having triumphed over our old nature and are restored to the right standing we held before the fall. In the name of Jesus, we come before your throne praying for a deeper understanding of what all this means. For more meaningful analysis of who we are in Christ and how that molds and shapes our identity. Let us no longer suffer from guilt and condemnation but

131

grant us revelation concerning the extraordinary life force that runs through our veins.

In the name of Jesus and finished work of the Cross, having been extended this precious gift to make amends at your throne, we no longer choose to live according to the course of this world. We have often called out on your name never grasping the full significance of what your name means. We failed to recognize the value of your Blood and the ancestry in which we were grafted. We repent for not embracing the true character of your Blood and the honorable priesthood in which we live. Please forgive us, Father, for refusing to shed our old nature and still holding on to the things of this world. In the name of Jesus, we come before you seeking a more intimate relationship with you putting aside our selfish wants and desires, for we are guilty of spiritual adultery by offering mere lip service and hypocrisy while holding onto carnal ways and doing those things which are not expedient, nor wise. We have justified our lifestyles and ignored your word, and our sins have found us out in the innermost parts of our hearts. For our faults and sin are not hidden from you. We have lived in rebellion and ignored your conviction while masquerading behind titles and the foolish praise of men. Now, Lord having thought about what this relationship truly means our hearts are heavy and we can no longer carry the guilt of our shame. We feel unworthy of your grace, and your mercy seems outside of our grip.

In the name of Jesus and the power of His Blood, we stand on your word, Father, that if we have faith the size of a mustard seed, we can move mountains. It was then, Lord, you spoke saying it only takes one drop of your Blood to make us whole. One drop of your Blood is enough to wash away years of remorse and failure. Although our shortcomings are many, our defeats too numerous to count and we have let you down time and time again; it only takes one drop of your Blood. Just one drop of your Blood to wash away the impurities of our hearts and the deterioration of our minds. One drop can restore our fellowship, renew our covenant, and replenish all that has been lost. No matter how hard the challenges we may face, how impossible our circumstances may seem, how long we have been without hope, and the years we have been defeated by darkness just one drop is all we need. It is in that vein we come before you, Heavenly Father, having been beaten to near submission, and on the edge of hopelessness that we urgently seek one drop.

To ask for more would be theft, but a faithful woman once said even the dogs eat the crumbs from their master's table. One drop of your Blood is as a mere crumb, but its power has greater value than countless goats and rams. One drop of your Blood and our tears can be turned to joy and the darkest moments of our past erased from the courts of Heaven and our convictions expunged. One drop of your Blood causes judgment to pass over, and the plague of sin and death have power no more. It is in this faith we set our petitions before you and cry out on your Blood. In the sincerity of our heart and acceptance of your abundant mercy, we pray for the strength to make a change and to head in a different direction. On the strength of one drop of your Blood, we ask for your help to turn away from all sin and the iniquity that has us bound. We no longer want to live as carnal Christians who bear your name but are absent of an honest and pure relationship with you. No longer walking in deception, blinded by darkness and devoid of your DNA. In the name of Jesus, we desire something more excellent than titles without power yet still being dead in our sins. We seek you, Lord, for a covenant and lineage in your family. You said our sins are forgotten as far as the east is from the west and we no longer carry the guilt and shame of our past. In the name of Jesus, we speak these words having a grain of faith and a drop of Blood believing you are not a man that you should lie, nor the son of man that you would deceive. We know and believe you are the Christ, the Son of the Living God, and we have access to your throne and inheritance in your Kingdom. Your word reminds us, Lord, how Jacob wrestled with an Angel to receive a blessing. He refused to let go and held on with all he had.

In the name of Jesus, let this prayer be the greatest of all prayers we have ever prayed. Let it be the line in the sand and the most coherent and deliberate words that have ever left our mouth. We come before you Lord with all respect and in great fear of your sovereign authority, standing on the word you authored, which said you put your word above your name. It is in that breathe and standing on that promise we refuse to leave without one drop. We stand in all boldness having faith in what you said, and after this prayer, nothing will ever be the same. After this prayer, we will inherit the DNA you died for and the promise of redemption through your blood. In this prayer, we are not merely seeking to be rescued from our mistakes and failures; rather; we are claiming deliverance with the expectation we will no longer see those issues again. We will be infused with your Blood that can renew our minds and heal our hearts of every wound and the rebellion we have harbored for so long. That all unforgiveness and bitterness will be washed away, and we will have a God consciousness choosing to do those things pleasing in your sight. In the name of Jesus and the power of His Blood, through this prayer we will no longer regard the consciousness of this world drifting further and further away from you, nor will we be moved by popular opinion and the worldly morals and values we are bombarded with each day. No longer will we seek the affirmation and approval of others when those things contradict and discredit who we are in Christ. We are immune to dark matter and low-frequency signals that attempt to gain access to our minds. In this prayer, you grant us the boldness to stand for righteousness regardless of the persecution it may bring and live a brand of Christianity that exalts Christ and the words He has spoken. In this prayer, our relationship with God will be defined by the Bible having faith; it is the unadulterated truth, and Christ is the head of our lives. He is the way, the truth, and the life and no man cometh to the Father but by Him. It is our faith, and our belief One Drop of His Blood can accomplish so much, and we will not be turned away by doubt and fear. We declare in His name we are dead to sin and in His eyes we stand without spot or blemish being granted compassion by the Father who deeply loves us. Believing for this purpose He graciously gave the Blood of His Son. Now thank you Lord for your parental guidance and instruction and for hearing and answering our prayers. In Jesus name, we pray. Thank God. Amen.

The Love of God

A common deception of Satan is distorting the meaning of God's love to negate the work of the cross and significance of Jesus Christ. It depicts God as a negligent parent who deprives His children of the most basic guidance, direction, and instructions in life. He would have us believe God imposes no boundaries or limitations on His children, tolerates all forms of disobedience, and has no concept of consequences and accountability. This "do as thou wilt" mentality is the premise of satanic worship and rebellion against God. It is a distorted view of love that substitutes the notion of a fallen nature in need of redemption with a belief we can live in whatever manner we please while still maintaining fellowship with God. It is based on the illusion God is obligated, as our creator, to cater to our needs and lustful desires while living our lives outside of His purpose and plan. We reduce God from being a loving Father who desires a relationship with His children to merely an agent or landlord who makes His rounds around the earth looking for opportunities to load us down with more gifts. Our lives of self-absorption, entitlement, and worldliness built on the premise the focus is on us as opposed to God. The whole notion of covenant, where God gives us His unconditional love, and we surrender all to Him, is lost in the idea God's love supersedes His commandments as opposed to God's love is His commandments.

This distorted perception has led many people to adopt the beliefs "God loves me too much to send me to Hell," and "God loves me the way I am" as foundations for living their lives. These statements are nothing more than justifications for continuing to live outside of the will of God and refusing to surrender all to Him. The first presumption is God is responsible for a person going to hell as opposed to Hell being a consequence of choice. The second based on the idea love is an excuse for sin and a justification for Heaven. In other words, God's love is a license to sin and a ticket to Heaven. The Bible states God's love is the gift of His Son Jesus Christ, and man's love is receiving Him as His Lord and Savior and being obedient to His word.

John 14:21 "He that hath my commandments, and keepeth them, he it is that loveth me: and he that loveth me shall be loved of my Father, and I will love him, and will manifest myself to him."

Revelation 22:14 "Blessed are they that do his commandments, that they may have right to the tree of life, and may enter in through the gates into the city."

John 3:18-20
3:18 "He that believeth on him is not condemned: but he that believeth not is condemned already, because he hath not believed in the name of the only begotten Son of God."
3:19 "And this is the condemnation, that light is come into the world, and men loved darkness rather than light, because their deeds were evil."
3:20 "For every one that doeth evil hateth the light, neither cometh to the light, lest his deeds should be reproved.

The Bible reassures us in no uncertain terms God loves man, but He hates sin, which can result in eternal separation from Him. Here is where the distinction made between the love of God and the judgment of God, which comes as a result of sin. There is nothing you can do to cause God to love you more or less than He already does. God is love, and since all men have sinned and come short of the glory of God, none of us have earned the right to be loved any more than our fellow man.

140

Romans 3:9-12

3:9 "What then? are we better than they? No, in no wise: for we have before proved both Jews and Gentiles, that they are all under sin;"

3:10 "As it is written, There is none righteous, no, not one:"

3:11 "There is none that understandeth, there is none that seeketh after God."

Romans 8 assures the believer nothing can separate us from God's love made available through Jesus Christ.

Romans 8:35-39

8:35 "Who shall separate us from the love of Christ? shall tribulation, or distress, or persecution, or famine, or nakedness, or peril, or sword?"

8:36 "As it is written, For thy sake we are killed all the day long; we are accounted as sheep for the slaughter."

8:37 "Nay, in all these things we are more than conquerors through him that loved us."

8:38 "For I am persuaded, that neither death, nor life, nor angels, nor principalities, nor powers, nor things present, nor things to come,"

8:39 "Nor height, nor depth, nor any other creature, shall be able to separate us from the love of God, which is in Christ Jesus our Lord."

Refusing Jesus Christ, by rejecting Him and His word, does not negate the love of God, but it will result in the judgment of sin and eternal separation from Him.

Ezekiel 18:4 "Behold, all souls are mine; as the soul of the father, so also the soul of the son is mine: the soul that sinneth, it shall die."

Romans 6:23 "For the wages of sin is death; but the gift of God is eternal life through Jesus Christ our Lord."

Galatians 5:19-21
5:19 "Now the works of the flesh are manifest, which are *these*; Adultery, fornication, uncleanness, lasciviousness,"
5:20 "Idolatry, witchcraft, hatred, variance, emulations, wrath, strife, seditions, heresies,"
5:21 "Envyings, murders, drunkenness, revellings, and such like: of the which I tell you before, as I have also told *you* in time past, that they which do such things shall not inherit the kingdom of God."

Throughout the Bible, are examples of God's judgment of sin and His loving efforts to warn His people to turn away from all iniquity. In the Old Testament, He sent prophets to inform the people of the inevitable judgment that would follow disobedience. In the New Testament, God sent His Son to be the final solution for sin by paying the ultimate price. The Word of God and His time-sensitive warnings concerning the final judgment of sin remains the same in both books. His judgment delayed because it is not His desire any man perishes, but all would repent and turn back to Him, but His judgment is sure, and all un-repented sin destroyed. We repent by accepting Jesus Christ as our Lord and Savior and turning away from sin. Only His blood can wash away our sins, and in Him, we have forgiveness and mercy for our shortcomings and weaknesses.

II Peter 3:9

3:9 "The Lord is not slack concerning his promise, as some men count slackness; but is longsuffering to us-ward, not willing that any should perish, but that all should come to repentance."

I John 1:9 "If we confess our sins, he is faithful and just to forgive us our sins, and to cleanse us from all unrighteousness."

All men feel God's love, and He is no respecter of persons. Everyone, the saint and sinner alike, benefits from His love. Evidenced by the fact the sun shines on the just and the unjust, air is breathed by the godly and ungodly, the rain does not discriminate when it waters the land, and Jesus Christ died on the cross for all men. God's love is full of grace, mercy, and compassion, but it is not a license to sin. God's love made Heaven a possibility, but it does not negate the reality of Hell. His love is laced with kindness and has a purpose in drawing men to Him, but He respects the rights of people who don't want to be drawn. In other words, just because good things happen in your life doesn't mean you won't be judged for your sin.

Matthew 5:45 "That ye may be the children of your Father which is in heaven: for he maketh his sun to rise on the evil and on the good, and sendeth rain on the just and on the unjust."

True love is a covenant, and one of the most significant examples of covenant was demonstrated by Jesus Christ in the "Garden of Gethsemane" moments before He was delivered to be crucified. His words, a declaration of total surrender, expressed an absolute commitment to God.

Matthew 26:39 "And he went a little further, and fell on his face, and prayed, saying, O my Father, if it be possible, let this cup pass from me: nevertheless not as I will, but as thou wilt."

His words depict the way we are supposed to reciprocate God's love. Jesus Christ was faithful unto death, and we are supposed to have the same mind.

Philippians 2:5-8
2:5 "Let this mind be in you, which was also in Christ Jesus:"
2:6 "Who, being in the form of God, thought it not robbery to be equal with God:"
2:7 "But made himself of no reputation, and took upon him the form of a servant, and was made in the likeness of men:"
2:8 "And being found in fashion as a man, he humbled himself, and became obedient unto death, even the death of the cross."

On the cross, Jesus sacrificed the most precious thing He had, which was not His life, but rather His fellowship with God. The Bible tells us He was one with His Father from the beginning of creation, but out of His willingness to please Him, He bore the sins of mankind causing Him to be out of fellowship with Him for the very first time. God is holy, and in Him is no darkness at all. Meaning despite His unconditional love for His son, He could not embrace the sin that was laid upon Him, for it is not possible for God to have any sin. The price Jesus paid for each one of us was echoed in those powerful words spoken on the cross, "My God, my God, why hast thou forsaken me?"

Matthew 27:46 "And about the ninth hour Jesus cried with a loud voice, saying, Eli, Eli, lama sabachthani?

that is to say, My God, my God, why hast thou forsaken me?"

We know this was God's Plan of redemption for man, but the point remains the love of God did not prevent Jesus from going to Hell, nor will it prevent those who live in rebellion from going. We also know God did not love Him the way He was and when the sins of man placed upon Him, God severed His fellowship with Him, until the work finished, and He received His Blood, the atonement for all sin. His Blood saves us from our sins, but to be covered by His Blood, you must repent and turn away from unrighteousness.

Hebrews 10:26-27
10:26 "For if we sin wilfully after that we have received the knowledge of the truth, there remaineth no more sacrifice for sins,"
10:27 "But a certain fearful looking for of judgment and fiery indignation, which shall devour the adversaries."

Being loved by God is not enough! He will not and cannot accept sin. The love of God has nothing to do with a person going to Hell and everything to do with a person not going. Sin will separate you from the

146

love of God and salvation through Jesus Christ is the only answer for sin. Jesus was manifested in the form of a man because He was the only one who could conquer sin, hell, and death by shedding His innocent Blood. The Bible tells us He was tempted in all points yet without sin. He was born of a virgin from the seed of God and untainted by the seed of man. He had the authority to destroy the works of Satan because He was unjustly charged and taken to Hell although He had done no wrong. He is the totality of God's love and the only way to escape the judgment which shall come upon all sin.

Hebrews 4:15 "For we have not an high priest which cannot be touched with the feeling of our infirmities; but was in all points tempted like as [we are, yet] without sin."

The Power to be Kept

There is nothing more powerful than the love of God, and once you receive salvation, He is faithful to help you every step of the way. There is eternal security in Him, and you don't have to live as if your relationship is on eggshells, but some people have the mistaken notion "once saved, always saved." In other words, your salvation is sealed from here to eternity once you give your life to Jesus Christ. They are led to believe once you confess Him as your Lord and Savior all you have to do is sit back and wait for Him to return, or die first, regardless to the choices you make in life. A nice thought, but without surrendering your heart to God, it is nothing more than a fantasy and catchphrase. We can allow our minds to become reprobate by choosing to chase after the things of this world and refusing to live by God's word. The very definition of an "Apostate" should put those thoughts to rest. A better notion is "once saved; you can be kept." God can save and keep you when you choose to remain in fellowship with Him.

John 14:23-24
14:23 "Jesus answered and said unto him, If a man love me, he will keep my words: and my Father will love him, and we will come unto him, and make our abode with him."
14:24 "He that loveth me not keepeth not my sayings: and the word which ye hear is not mine, but the Father's which sent me."

Matthew 24:13 "But he that shall endure unto the end, the same shall be saved."

Romans 8:16-17
8:16 "The Spirit itself beareth witness with our spirit, that we are the children of God:"
8:17 "And if children, then heirs; heirs of God, and joint-heirs with Christ; if so be that we suffer with *him*, that we may be also glorified together."

The Bible warns us in the days preceding the return of Jesus Christ; many will fall away from the faith. To slip away, you must have once been a part of the Body of Christ and subsequently departed. Again, God never takes away our right to choose even after we confess Jesus Christ as our Savior.

I Timothy 4:1 "Now the Spirit speaketh expressly, that in the latter times some shall depart from the faith, giving heed to seducing spirits, and doctrines of devils;

II Thessalonians 2:3 "Let no man deceive you by any means: for that day shall not come, except there come a falling away first, and that man of sin be revealed, the son of perdition;"

It is essential to understand giving your life to God does not mean everything is going to be perfect from that moment forward. You may experience setbacks and battle sin, but you must continue to consciously and deliberately seek Him for help and strength. Your life may be consumed with repentance, and your victories may be far and few in between, but He is faithful and will never leave or forsake you. That means honestly acknowledging your faults and making a sincere effort to turn away from sin as opposed to embracing and making excuses for it. Being kept requires effort and a sincere heart. Jesus Christ paid the price for sin, but when you reject the truth and refuse to repent your heart is hardened, and sin becomes rebellion. Rebellion is not covered by His Blood, which results in God's judgment instead of His mercy.

Hebrews 10:26 "For if we sin wilfully after that we have received the knowledge of the truth, there remaineth no more sacrifice for sins,"

Hebrews 12:1-2

12:1 "Wherefore seeing we also are compassed about with so great a cloud of witnesses, let us lay aside every weight, and the sin which doth so easily beset *us*, and let us run with patience the race that is set before us," 12:2 "Looking unto Jesus the author and finisher of *our* faith; who for the joy that was set before him endured the cross, despising the shame, and is set down at the right hand of the throne of God."

Let's be clear. There is absolutely nothing we can do to earn salvation or give God to repay Him for what He has given us. We do not get into Heaven because of how good we have been, things we have accomplished, people we have helped, sacrifices we have made, or people we have led to Christ. Neither does our title in the church, the praise and esteem of others, awards we have won, spiritual gifts we possess, money we have accumulated, the amount of our tithes and offerings, how much time we have studied and prayed, or the number of church services we have attended earn our salvation. We can only receive salvation by God's grace and mercy. It is an unmerited gift obtained through His Only Begotten Son, Jesus Christ. Considering this undisputed fact, every believer in Christ must also understand **"what we do once we**

receive salvation matters." In other words, works can't save you, but they are the best indicator of where you are in Christ, or whether you even belong to Christ at all. The danger of claiming mercy while living outside of the will of God is rolling the dice where salvation is concerned. The Bible says many will stand before the Lord at The Day of Judgment only to discover their heart was never with Him despite the words they uttered out of their mouth. Again, what you do now is a good indicator of where you will end up later.

Matthew 7:21-23
7:21 "Not every one that saith unto me, Lord, Lord, shall enter into the kingdom of heaven; but he that doeth the will of my Father which is in heaven."
7:22 "Many will say to me in that day, Lord, Lord, have we not prophesied in thy name? and in thy name have cast out devils? and in thy name done many wonderful works?"
7:23 "And then will I profess unto them, I never knew you: depart from me, ye that work iniquity."

Matthew 15:7-8
15:7 "*Ye* hypocrites, well did Esaias prophesy of you, saying,"
15: 8 "This people draweth nigh unto me with their mouth, and honoureth me with *their* lips; but their heart is far from me."

Since the fall of man, God spoke a plan of salvation for every man, woman, and child to be redeemed back to Him. This plan included a means by which each of us could achieve this end. Within this plan, the road to Heaven paved, our Savior prepared, our mansions in Heaven built, our callings and purposes predetermined, the rapture date set, and preparations finalized for the marriage supper of the Lamb. A chair placed at the table of the feast for every man, woman, and child, but it has always been conditioned upon choice and free will.

The key word is "choice." Choice distinguishes man from the rest of God's creatures. He entrusted man with the awesome responsibility to choose his fate. God spoke His will into the earth, including what He purposed to accomplish, but conditioned it upon man's right to choose. We never lose the right to decide to come into agreement with His will. Do you think it was the will of God for Adam to disobey Him in the garden? Do you think it was God's will for David to sleep with Bathsheba and have her husband killed? Was it the will of God for Moses to strike the rock instead of

153

speaking to it? Of course not, but man's right to choose supersedes the will of God because God afforded him this right.

To be kept, you must choose to live by the word of God to the best of your ability. The word is our blueprint to Heaven and to live contrary to it results in devastation, loss, and ultimately eternal darkness. To be kept, you must have total reliance on the word of God. You cannot separate God from His word. Through the Bible, God molds and shapes us into His children. To be kept, you must study His word for guidance and direction.

Proverbs 16:25 "There is a way that seemeth right unto a man, but the end thereof *are* the ways of death."

Hebrews 4:12 "For the word of God *is* quick, and powerful, and sharper than any twoedged sword, piercing even to the dividing asunder of soul and spirit, and of the joints and marrow, and *is* a discerner of the thoughts and intents of the heart."

To be kept, you must live separate from the world's system of rebellion against God. When the Bible talks about the world, it is referring to everything operating outside of the design, will, and plan of God. It

154

is a diabolical system controlled by Satan, the god of
this world, motivated by man's desires as opposed to
God's will.

II Corinthians 4:3-4
4:3 "But if our gospel be hid, it is hid to them that are
lost:"
4:4 "In whom the god of this world hath blinded the
minds of them which believe not, lest the light of the
glorious gospel of Christ, who is the image of God,
should shine unto them.

The world is characterized by the ungodly influences
and lustful images we are bombarded with each day
while attacking any notions of Biblical values and
morality. It calls those things which are evil good and
those things which are good evil. This is based on
man's arrogance and self-will as opposed to the Word
and Revelation of God. It is a slippery slope leading us
quickly down the path of a "do as thou wilt mentality"
fueled by the manipulated masses believing they are as
gods and free to do as they please. The entire system is
willfully ignorant and driven by the lust of the flesh, the
lust of the eyes, and the pride of life as people blatantly
ignore the truth right before them.

I John 2:15-16

2:15 "Love not the world, neither the things *that are* in the world. If any man love the world, the love of the Father is not in him."

2:16 "For all that *is* in the world, the lust of the flesh, and the lust of the eyes, and the pride of life, is not of the Father, but is of the world."

2:17 "And the world passeth away, and the lust thereof: but he that doeth the will of God abideth for ever."

The Bible warns us not to be brought under the world's influence, nor should we give in to its temptations and divers lust.

Romans 12:1-2

12:1 "I beseech you therefore, brethren, by the mercies of God, that ye present your bodies a living sacrifice, holy, acceptable unto God, *which is* your reasonable service."

12:2 "And be not conformed to this world: but be ye transformed by the renewing of your mind, that ye may prove what *is* that good, and acceptable, and perfect, will of God."

To be kept, we must die to our old nature, or old characteristics and ways of thinking, and make a firm decision not to partake in those activities that are ungodly or can lead to ungodliness. You cannot act like the world, think like the world, or participate in lustful pleasures with the world and expect to stay in fellowship with God. Living for Christ is a daily decision to align yourself with the things of God and no longer participate in behaviors that oppose, contradict, diminish, and discredit His Word. It is a choice not to compromise the things of God or to justify and rationalize sin regardless of the tough decisions made. The more you grow in Christ and learn about His nature, the more selective you become about where you go, what you watch and listen to, influences you allow in your life, what you support and stand for, and with whom you are in fellowship and agreement. That is why it is every Christian's responsibility to learn more about God, spend time with Him in the Word and prayer, and develop a personal and intimate relationship with Him.

There is no peace in the world for a child of God because the light of Christ is in direct opposition with the dark spirit in the world. When Jesus came across people possessed by the devil, the demonic spirits in them recognized who He was, so if Christ is in you, they will recognize Him. In other words, demonic spirits will attack, despise and torment you to drown out your light. A child of God takes a severe beating when he/she lives on both sides of the fence. Ultimately, compromising can cost you your soul because, over time, the spiritual beatings you endure will suffocate your light and strip you of everything. Have you ever wondered why it seems like people in the world are bold and appear to be having the times of their lives, but the moment you try, it results in disastrous consequences? A child of God only has the illusion of fitting in the world.

Mark 1:23-24
1:23 "And there was in their synagogue a man with an unclean spirit; and he cried out,"
1:24 "Saying, Let *us* alone; what have we to do with thee, thou Jesus of Nazareth? art thou come to destroy us? I know thee who thou art, the Holy One of God."

To be Kept, you must understand what the Bible says about giving and receiving forgiveness. The power of forgiveness is activated the moment you decide to accept Jesus Christ as your Lord and Savior. Accept the fact even though none of us deserved the pardon, nor could we afford to pay the price ourselves, Jesus paid it all. You cannot earn forgiveness; you receive it and release it in the lives of others because the Blood of

Jesus is more significant than our sin. If you refuse to forgive others, He will not forgive you.

Matthew 6:14-15
6:14 "For if ye forgive men their trespasses, your heavenly Father will also forgive you:"
6:15 "But if ye forgive not men their trespasses, neither will your Father forgive your trespasses."

There was a time in each of our lives we walked in darkness, alienated from the knowledge and revelation of Christ, until that day our eyes opened, and we allowed Him into our hearts. Indeed, the road leading to salvation is riddled with cruel and wicked acts, selfishness, scandal, betrayal, insensitivity, cold and callous thoughts, and an assortment of deviant and rebellious behavior. It can be very tough to overcome the thought "we deserve to be punished for what we have done," when receiving forgiveness and letting go of condemnation and guilt from our past. The whole concept of mercy can appear to be irresponsible and unfair to those we have hurt and caused so much pain. Guilt becomes our way of making it right by embracing the pain as a form of punishment for our sins. It's even harder when we are still challenged by various

159

shortcomings in our lives even after we have received Jesus Christ and believed on Him for deliverance.

Romans 8:1 *"There is* therefore now no condemnation to them which are in Christ Jesus, who walk not after the flesh, but after the Spirit.

Forgiveness is not without accountability. I often tell people, "You never get away with anything." Everything you do in life has consequences. God does not excuse us from our behavior; rather; He points out the error of our ways while drawing us to repentance. In His grace, we endeavor to make things right. His favor and love can straighten our path, repair what has been broken, restore what has been lost, redeem the time, heal emotions, and renew our way of thinking, but it does not erase what we have done and the pain we have caused others. Indeed, the Blood of Jesus can deliver us from our past and wipes our slate clean, but while we live upon the earth, we reap what we sow. The Bible says He remembers our sin no more meaning we stand before Him redeemed by the Blood of His Son. However, it may take years to repair the damage you have caused here on earth. The whole notion of Heavenly crowns and rewards lets us know what you do in the earth matters. Strive to be free of sin and learn from your mistakes. The goal should always be to have victory over sin while knowing forgiveness is available to help us in this journey. His love and His compassion will lead, guide, and direct our way, and we are kept only if our heart is sincere.

An essential part of forgiveness is repentance, which involves more than just words. Too often, people adopt the belief it is merely verbalizing the wrongs they committed. True repentance builds character, sincerity, and honesty and involves a commitment to correcting the offensive behavior. It is a condition of the heart requiring examination accompanied by change. It requires you to acknowledge any shortcomings, failures, problems, issues, stumbling blocks, or hindrances in your life and allowing the Word of God to work on those areas not lined up with His will. Repentance is a good indicator of the true intentions of the heart. Be willing to address those things within your control. Apologize to those you offended, hurt, or harmed, restore what you have taken by fraud or deceit, take responsibility for bad decisions and lapses in judgment, and be accountable to those you owe accountability.

Luke 19:8 "And Zacchaeus stood, and said unto the Lord; Behold, Lord, the half of my goods I give to the poor; and if I have taken any thing from any man by false accusation, I restore *him* fourfold."

The ministry of Jesus Christ is built on repentance. The Bible says the truth will set you free, but often the truth hurts and is hard to accept. For this cause, the Bible warns us not to think of ourselves more highly than we ought since we are born in sin and shaped in iniquity. In other words, we have all sinned and come short of the Glory of God. We all have some ugly and uncomfortable things to deal with in our lives and should appreciate the opportunity to repent and receive the Lord's help in turning away from those things.

1 John 1:9 "If we confess our sins, he is faithful and just to forgive us *our* sins, and to cleanse us from all unrighteousness."

Hebrews 8:12 "For I will be merciful to their unrighteousness, and their sins and their iniquities will I remember no more."

The danger today is many people base their standing with God upon their outward success, a distorted view of God's love, and erroneous catchphrases, as opposed to the actual condition of his/her heart. Repentance requires looking inward first and being honest about your real motives and intentions. Do you seek to be rescued or delivered? Do you only want the pain to go away, or are you completely ready to walk away from those things causing you pain? Do you want your situation to be better, or are you looking for a better situation? Consider the following scripture the next time you hide behind the phrase "God knows my heart," as opposed to allowing God to change your heart.

Jeremiah 17: 9 "The heart *is* deceitful above all *things*, and desperately wicked: who can know it?

Allowing God to deal with your heart opens the door for real prosperity, healing, and deliverance. The fact sin got in is one thing (protect your mind, and guard your heart), but the more significant issue is allowing it to remain in your life. Repentance is not a quick fix; it is about changing your life. In the next passage of scriptures concerning the two men on the cross next to Jesus, one man sought nothing more than to save his life and the other man sought salvation even if it cost him his life. In other words, some people are just looking for a way off the cross as opposed to the way to eternal life.

Luke 23:39-43

23:39 "And one of the malefactors which were hanged railed on him, saying, If thou be Christ, save thyself and us."

23:40 "But the other answering rebuked him, saying, Dost not thou fear God, seeing thou art in the same condemnation?"

23:41 "And we indeed justly; for we receive the due reward of our deeds: but this man hath done nothing amiss."

23:42 "And he said unto Jesus, Lord, remember me when thou comest into thy kingdom."

23:43 "And Jesus said unto him, Verily I say unto thee, To day shalt thou be with me in paradise."

In scripture, Jesus not only forgave men. He explicitly instructed them to "sin no more." In other words, He told them to repent and turn away from the offensive behavior or act. Sin will utterly destroy your life. It will rob you of everything and significantly impair your relationships. It results in bad decisions, missed opportunities, and devastation and pain in your life and the lives of others. It can lead to sickness, depression, paranoia, fear, and even death. We see families that are destroyed by the actions of others, resulting in harm to those they were supposed to take care of and love. We observe how selfishness drives people to abandon their marriages and make decisions that scar others for years to come. Again, sin is a destroyer and the more of it you have in your life, the more devastating the consequences.

John 5:14 "Afterward Jesus findeth him in the temple, and said unto him, Behold, thou art made whole: sin no more, lest a worse thing come unto thee."

Sin is cancer with only one cure, "The Blood of Jesus." I say this to emphasize the point forgiveness is a gift not abused. It is not a license to sin and live outside of the will of God, merely asking for forgiveness after the fact. There are too many people today that justify sin and embrace their fallen nature as opposed to battling it. The result is a sinful lifestyle which keeps them trapped in their fallen nature. To be kept, you must honestly deal with the sin in your life.

__Prayer__

God the Father, Eternal God and Father of Lights. Lord
of Host who is not a million miles away, but right here
with us each day, able to hear our petitions and willing
to help us in our time of need. Just and Righteous God
whose word is sure and commandments are not
grievous. In the name of your Only Begotten Son, Jesus
Christ, Spirit of Wisdom and Understanding, we come
before your great and holy throne declaring our undying
faith in your word. We stand on your sure and precious
promises, knowing you place your word above your
name. It will not return unto you void, but accomplish
all you please, and prosper in the thing where you sent
it. In the name of Jesus and the power of His Blood, we
ask, Lord, that you will have compassion on us,
according to your loving kindness and the multitude of
thy tender mercies. We stand before your throne, Lord,
naked before the truth and guilty as charged. We
acknowledge our transgressions before you, and our sin
is not hidden from your sight for we were shaped in
iniquity and in sin were we conceived. In the name of

Jesus and the power of His Blood, we acknowledge our shortcomings and weaknesses and confess any sin in our lives, both known and unknown. We humble ourselves and ask you to examine the hidden places of our hearts and the most remote areas of our minds, holding back nothing and revealing all things to you. In the name of Jesus, we ask you to examine our motives and the intentions of our heart and let us live righteously in your sight. Grant us a heart to turn away from all rebellion and anything not lined up with your will and help us to be easily convicted and quick to get things right with you. For you are the Creator and we are clay in your hands. In the name of Jesus, we trust you, Heavenly Father, to cleanse us from all unrighteousness and establish us in the truth. In Jesus name, we pray. Thank God. Amen.

Crossroads For Deception

II Thessalonians 2:3 "Let no man deceive you by any means: for *that day shall not come,* except there come a falling away first, and that man of sin be revealed, the son of perdition;"

Jeremiah 5:26 "For among my people are found wicked men: they lay wait, as he that setteth snares; they set a trap, they catch men."

Matthew 24:11 "And many false prophets shall arise and deceive many"

Jude 1:4 "For there are certain men crept in unawares, who were before of old ordained to this condemnation, ungodly men, turning the grace of our God into lasciviousness, and denying the only Lord God, and our Lord Jesus Christ."

Our revelation of Jesus Christ is the foundation for our relationship with God. It is our anchor in the face of doubt and adversity. It is a living, breathing experience with a Savior whose words are alive and authority spans from the beginning until the end.

Revelation 12:11 "And they overcame him by the blood of the Lamb, and by the word of their testimony; and they loved not their lives unto the death."

Knowing God for yourself is the realization we have an individual appointment with Him and must be ready to give a personal account of the life we lived. It is a firm decision to serve Him with all your heart, mind, body, soul, and spirit even if you are the only person in the universe who chooses to do so. It is the belief the Word of God is not validated by the approval and affirmations of men but is absolute truth, accurate in every assertion, and infallible in the totality of its shape and design. It means even if prominent leaders fall you will not fall with them, if your neighbors go after idols, you will not go down the same path, and if the entire nation veers from His instruction, your foot is steadfast and shall not be moved. In other words, there may be times in life when it appears you are alone, and the whole world stands against you, but your faith is not deterred.

Joshua 24:15 "And if it seem evil unto you to serve the LORD, choose you this day whom ye will serve; whether the gods which your fathers served that were on the other side of the flood, or the gods of the Amorites, in whose land ye dwell: but as for me and my house, we will serve the LORD."

Romans 3:3-4

3:3 "For what if some did not believe? shall their unbelief make the faith of God without effect?
3:4 "God forbid: yea, let God be true, but every man a liar; as it is written, That thou mightest be justified in thy sayings, and mightest overcome when thou art judged."

Despite the days we are in, God has a remnant of men and women who will remain faithful until the very end. He has anointed people in leadership positions who are surrendered to His will and teach how to rely on the Word of God. We should hold them in high esteem, love, encourage, support and pray for them. Humble servants who seek neither fame nor fortune, are motivated by a sincere desire to be used by Him and give Him all the glory, praise, and honor. They teach their members how to have a personal relationship with Him, recognizing their authority ends where their opinion begins. These true Ambassadors of the Lord Jesus Christ represent Him in the earth and are committed to lifting Him up as opposed to making a name for themselves. They are not afraid to preach God's word, which provokes, convicts, and challenges people to change their ungodly ways. They are not interested in entertaining the masses seeking to win souls as opposed to drawing large crowds. Discipleship, not membership, is their goal and they understand they were sent to serve the people as opposed to being served by them.

Ephesians 4:11-12
4:11 "And he gave some, apostles; and some, prophets; and some, evangelists; and some, pastors and teachers;" 4:12 "For the perfecting of the saints, for the work of the ministry, for the edifying of the body of Christ:"

Isaiah 62:6 "I have set watchmen upon thy walls, O Jerusalem, which shall never hold their peace day nor night: ye that make mention of the LORD, keep not silence,"

Jeremiah 3:15 "And I will give you pastors according to mine heart, which shall feed you with knowledge and understanding."

Hebrews 10:17 "Obey them that have the rule over you, and submit yourselves: for they watch for your souls, as they that must give account, that they may do it with joy, and not with grief: for that [is] unprofitable for you."

The church has great significance to God, and the Bible instructs us to come together with other believers, the importance of accountability and having a

171

faithful shepherd to provide spiritual guidance to the flock. It is unwise to adopt the belief you can teach yourself or rely on the internet for instruction as opposed to finding a good church and Pastor. In legal circles it is said "he that represents himself has a fool for a client" highlighting the importance of obtaining competent counsel when faced with legal issues. The same said of those who have abandoned the church and see no need for spiritual leadership and instruction. The Bible does not support such a decision, and your personal relationship with God must be balanced with the need for fellowship, sound counsel, encouragement, ethical guidance, and teaching.

Romans 10:14-15
10:14 "How then shall they call on him in whom they have not believed? and how shall they believe in him of whom they have not heard? and how shall they hear without a preacher?"
10:15 "And how shall they preach, except they be sent? as it is written, How beautiful are the feet of them that preach the gospel of peace, and bring glad tidings of good things!"

Hebrews 10:23-25
10:23 "Let us hold fast the profession of *our* faith without wavering; (for he *is* faithful that promised;)"

10:24 "And let us consider one another to provoke unto love and to good works:"
10:25 "Not forsaking the assembling of ourselves together, as the manner of some *is*; but exhorting *one another*: and so much the more, as ye see the day approaching."

The Bible also warns we live in a day of great deception and the church is not immune from men who exploit the flock and fail to feed them the Word of God. Satan himself appears as an angel of light and righteousness, and it is no marvel if his ministers do the same. He was present in the Garden of Eden, and he is very active in the church today. When leaders stray away from the Bible, they become vulnerable to the same psychology and reasoning which caused Adam to fall.

False prophets operate as wolves in sheep's clothing. They have self-serving agendas and motives, bring in false doctrines, and cause the people to chase after vain things. They make merchandise of the people, exploiting them, perverting the gospel, and consumed with lust and greed. They neither warn the people concerning the judgments of God nor teach them to obey His statutes and commandments. Instead of

173

teaching their members how to come out of the world, they promise them more of its pleasures, capitalizing on their fears, lust, and insecurities. They deny the Lord Jesus Christ is the only way; dispute the existence of Hell and the virgin birth and cast doubt the Bible is the unadulterated Word of God. They come from various denominations, in all shapes and sizes, from the storefront to the megachurch, claiming to have supernatural knowledge only they can understand, and revelation so deep not even the Bible can contain it. They are gifted speakers who will have you believe there is another chapter after the book of Revelation or book before Genesis. Men and women of great charisma and influence who appeal to the emotion of their listeners doing nothing more than tickling their ears while leaving them scripturally defunct.

II. Timothy 4:1-4
4:1 "I charge thee therefore before God, and the Lord Jesus Christ, who shall judge the quick and the dead at his appearing and his kingdom;"
4:2 "Preach the word; be instant in season, out of season; reprove, rebuke, exhort with all longsuffering and doctrine."

4:3 "For the time will come when they will not endure sound doctrine; but after their own lusts shall they heap to themselves teachers, having itching ears;"
4:4 "And they shall turn away their ears from the truth, and shall be turned unto fables."

II Peter 2:1-3
2:1 "But there were false prophets also among the people, even as there shall be false teachers among you, who privily shall bring in damnable heresies, even denying the Lord that bought them, and bring upon themselves swift destruction."
2:2 "And many shall follow their pernicious ways; by reason of whom the way of truth shall be evil spoken of."
2:3 "And through covetousness shall they with feigned words make merchandise of you: whose judgment now of a long time lingereth not, and their damnation slumbereth not."

Instead of advocating a relationship with Jesus Christ, as defined by the Bible, these false prophets promote religion without rules. The result is justifications like "I have my own relationship with God," as an exemption to living according to the Bible. They distort the Word and do away with notions of accountability and consequences for sin. Through their watered-down preaching, they attempt to bring God down to the level of man, and the more common He

175

becomes, the less fear and reverence the people have towards Him. They enjoy access to pulpits and Christian media, are held in high esteem, hold leadership positions throughout the church, and are followed by many mesmerized by their talents, gifts, and abilities. In other words, they appear to be as beautiful, wise, and gifted as Lucifer, who is the source of their power and strength.

The Bible warns us in the days preceding the return of Jesus Christ there will be a great falling away from the faith as many deceivers shall rise to turn the hearts of the people away from the truth. We are in those days, and the devil knows his time is short. He is waging a more aggressive campaign against the church. We see the emergence of a new definition of Christianity so vague and inclusive; it doesn't require adherence to the Bible nor acceptance of the divinity and purpose of Christ. Under the guise of love, peace, inclusion, and equality He will promote leaders who water down the gospel, question the infallible nature of the Bible, and turn their members away from the absolute certainty of salvation through none other than Jesus Christ.

Revelation 12:12 "Therefore rejoice, ye heavens, and ye that dwell in them. Woe to the inhabiters of the earth and of the sea! for the devil is come down unto you, having great wrath, because he knoweth that he hath but a short time."

II Corinthians 11:13-15
11:13 "For such *are* false apostles, deceitful workers, transforming themselves into the apostles of Christ."
11:14 "And no marvel; for Satan himself is transformed into an angel of light."
11:15 "Therefore *it is* no great thing if his ministers also be transformed as the ministers of righteousness; whose end shall be according to their works."

Lucifer was created a musical masterpiece, having tabrets and pipes prepared within, and can create a religious ceremony that moves both the body and mind. Because we were created with a revelation of God inside of us, he understands our need to fill this void, so he uses religion and mysticism to create a counterfeit experience. Satan works to mimic God and loves an entertaining church service where no Word is taught. He will dance, shout, shed tears, clap, stir the crowd into a frenzy, fall out, and sing in the choir

177

because emotion and motivational speeches are no threat to him or his kingdom. It's like firing a cap gun at a lion because only the truth of God's Word can set you free. Attending a church without truth is no different than an electrifying rock concert minus the sound effects and pyrotechnics. At least, no sound effects and pyrotechnics yet.

Many people are deceived because they are chasing gifts instead of pursuing God. They are making decisions about leaders based on their talents and abilities as opposed to their lifestyles and obedience to the Word of God. They are making rock stars out of men because they can preach and sing. The Bible says gifts and callings are irrevocable, meaning they can be used for His purpose and glory or your purpose. You could preach the walls down and sing with the voice of angels, and not be in fellowship with God. The devil can do all these things, but he can't live "the life." Therefore, the Bible warns us to know a person by their fruits, or way they live their lives, not their gifts. Fruits are the evidence of a surrendered life, meaning you practice what you preach and give all the glory and honor to Him. God's glory is for Him alone, therefore; people should see Him in your life before they see your gift.

Romans 11:29 "For the gifts and calling of God *are* without repentance."

Isaiah 42:8 "I *am* the LORD: that *is* my name: and my glory will I not give to another, neither my praise to graven images.

Matthew 7:15-20
7:15 "Beware of false prophets, which come to you in sheep's clothing, but inwardly they are ravening wolves."
7:16 "Ye shall know them by their fruits. Do men gather grapes of thorns, or figs of thistles?"
7:17 "Even so every good tree bringeth forth good fruit; but a corrupt tree bringeth forth evil fruit."
7:18 "A good tree cannot bring forth evil fruit, neither *can* a corrupt tree bring forth good fruit."
7:19 "Every tree that bringeth not forth good fruit is hewn down, and cast into the fire."
7:20 "Wherefore by their fruits ye shall know them."

The Bible instructs us in no uncertain terms to keep ourselves untainted by the influence of the world and to stand for righteousness. We are told not to adopt the ways of this world or go after idols and false gods. Today, some churches not only embrace the world's culture but refuse to preach against their practices as well. Many times, out of a deceptive belief if we become more accommodating to the world, we can win them to Christ, and other times through compromise, self-ambition, and justifications. The more we embrace the culture of the world, the more distorted and watered down the church becomes. In our efforts to attract the world and fill the seats, we give secular celebrities access to tremendous resources and opportunities within the church, use their names as headliners to boost attendance and draw people to events, and validate them in the eyes of our members without seeing fruit they are saved. Satan operates undetected because the focus is on the talents and gifts as opposed to lifestyle and fruit. They have the appearance of Christ, but their hearts are full of rebellion and iniquity. We sing with them, dance with them, and it becomes a profitable situation for all parties involved. It is this sort of hypocrisy causing us to lose our identity and allowing the world to define us. The greatest threat to Christianity today is hypocritical Christians. It's bad advertisement, and even the world knows better than that. God's word has not changed, and the Bible tells us to flee from all appearances of evil not to embrace it and call it blessed. At the core, it's wanting to be like the world, embracing their standards of prosperity and success, and sharing their spotlight and stage, as opposed to preaching the truth and seeing them delivered and won to Christ.

Proverbs 1:10 "My son if sinners entice thee, consent thou not."

Matthew 7:21-23
7:21 "Not every one that saith unto me, Lord, Lord, shall enter into the kingdom of heaven; but he that doeth the will of my Father which is in heaven."
7:22 "Many will say to me in that day, Lord, Lord, have we not prophesied in thy name? and in thy name have cast out devils? and in thy name done many wonderful works?"
7:23 "And then will I profess unto them, I never knew you: depart from me, ye that work iniquity."

Matthew 15:7-9
15:7 "*Ye* hypocrites, well did Esaias prophesy of you, saying,"
15:8 "This people draweth nigh unto me with their mouth, and honoureth me with *their* lips; but their heart is far from me."
15:9 "But in vain they do worship me, teaching *for* doctrines the commandments of men."

II. Corinthians 6:14-17

6:14 "Be ye not unequally yoked together with unbelievers: for what fellowship hath righteousness with unrighteousness? and what communion hath light with darkness?"

6:15 "And what concord hath Christ with Belial? or what part hath he that believeth with an infidel?"

6:16 "And what agreement hath the temple of God with idols? for ye are the temple of the living God; as God hath said, I will dwell in them, and walk in them; and I will be their God, and they shall be my people."

6:17 "Wherefore come out from among them, and be ye separate, saith the Lord, and touch not the unclean thing; and I will receive you,"

6:18 "And will be a Father unto you, and ye shall be my sons and daughters, saith the Lord Almighty."

Satan is the god of this world, and the riches of this world are at his disposal. He is not all-powerful but exercises authority in this realm. He attempts to destroy us from the inside out by drawing us into rebellion and out of fellowship with God. Remember how mighty the nation of Israel was because God fought their battles. No other nation could stand before them, so Satan surrounded them with the ungodly influences of the people around them. When Israel embraced their wicked customs and went after their gods, they no longer operated in the authority and protection of God and were defeated by their enemies. The church is no different and the more we water down the things of God by embracing the customs of the world, the more susceptible we are to the same fate. The only defense against satanic deception is holiness and walking in obedience to the Lord.

Revelation 2:14 "But I have a few things against thee, because thou hast there them that hold the doctrine of Balaam, who taught Balac to cast a stumblingblock before the children of Israel, to eat things sacrificed unto idols, and to commit fornication."

Jesus Christ is the same yesterday, today, and forever, and the Bible tells us it is God who draws men unto Him, not gimmicks, entertainment, and big names. The same anointing which resulted in countless people delivered, healed and made whole wherever He went, and the same anointing which fell on the disciples on the Day of Pentecost resulting in three thousand souls added to the Kingdom is still available today. He did not compromise the will of God to win souls unto Him, and we do not have to compromise holiness, reverence, and the fear of God to win people to Christ. We need to live according to the word of God while demonstrating

His love and compassion. We are trying too hard to be friends with the world. Instead of showing them a better way, we are feeding them the same stuff they're bound with merely repackaging the lifestyles and lyrics and calling it Jesus. The Word is what draws men to Jesus, not outward things.

John 6:44 "No man can come to me, except the Father which hath sent me draw him: and I will raise him up at the last day."

Hebrews 13:8 "Jesus Christ the same yesterday, and today, and for ever."

When you live for God sacrifices must be made, some stages you will never see, interviews you will never get, events you will not be invited too, friends you will not have, success you will never achieve, fame you will never reach, and crowds you will not see. You will receive persecution instead of popularity and conviction instead of affirmation. To live for Christ is to suffer with Him and if the world hated Him, why do they love you so much? If you genuinely represent Christ, then they will treat you the same way they treated Him. You see no one gets a free pass to just smile and preach the nice stuff while others are ostracized and ridiculed for standing on the Word. The very essence of preaching the gospel in a dying world is it will either convict you to change or offend those who choose to remain the same. To stay silent in the face of being unpopular is to deny the very Lord you claim to love. Just as you will not make a stand for Him on earth, He will not make a stand for you in Heaven. Those who suffer with Him shall also reign with Him meaning His family is those who are not ashamed of Him and His words.

John 15:18-20
15:18 "If the world hate you, ye know that it hated me before *it hated* you."
15:19 "If ye were of the world, the world would love his own: but because ye are not of the world, but I have chosen you out of the world, therefore the world hateth you."
15:20 "Remember the word that I said unto you, The servant is not greater than his lord. If they have persecuted me, they will also persecute you; if they have kept my saying, they will keep yours also."

John 3:18-21
3:18 "He that believeth on him is not condemned: but he that believeth not is condemned already, because he hath not believed in the name of the only begotten Son of God."

3:19 "And this is the condemnation, that light is come into the world, and men loved darkness rather than light, because their deeds were evil."
3:20 "For every one that doeth evil hateth the light, neither cometh to the light, lest his deeds should be reproved."
3:21 "But he that doeth truth cometh to the light, that his deeds may be made manifest, that they are wrought in God."

James 4:4 "Ye adulterers and adulteresses, know ye not that the friendship of the world is enmity with God? whosoever therefore will be a friend of the world is the enemy of God."

Matthew 6:24 "No man can serve two masters: for either he will hate the one, and love the other; or else he will hold to the one, and despise the other. Ye cannot serve God and mammon.

II Timothy 2:12 "If we suffer, we shall also reign with *him*: if we deny *him*, he also will deny us:"

Mark 8:38 "Whosoever therefore shall be ashamed of me and of my words in this adulterous and sinful generation; of him also shall the Son of man be ashamed, when he cometh in the glory of his Father with the holy angels."

The Bible warns us the deceit will become so pervasive and intense the very elect deceived if they are not careful. Meaning, it doesn't matter how long you have been in the church, how many times you have read the Bible, or your position and titles, the minute you stray away from the Word of God you will become a casualty of war. Don't be fooled by the accolades and affirmation of men, the size of the sanctuary, or the number of people who fill the seats; man is no match for Satan and the wisdom he possesses. He is meticulous and patient like the moving of the earth unseen by the naked eye. He will lose to make you think your winning and watch you rise to great heights to ensure the magnitude and impact of your fall. When He tempted Jesus in the wilderness, the Lord did not veer from the Word responding, "It is Written," and Michael, the Archangel, when disputing with Satan stated, "The Lord rebuke you!" Today we see leaders driven by big ideas and marketing strategies, as opposed to the unadulterated Word of God.

Luke 4:6-8
4:6 "And the devil said unto him, All this power will I give thee, and the glory of them: for that is delivered unto me; and to whomsoever I will I give it."
4:7 "If thou therefore wilt worship me, all shall be thine."

4:8 "And Jesus answered and said unto him, Get thee behind me, Satan: for it is written, Thou shalt worship the Lord thy God, and him only shalt thou serve."

Jude 1:9 "Yet Michael the archangel, when contending with the devil he disputed about the body of Moses, durst not bring against him a railing accusation, but said, The Lord rebuke thee.

As discussed in previous chapters, we are witnessing the grand finale of Satan's plan which dates to Heaven where he deceived 1/3 of the Angelic host to join in his rebellion against the Most High God. He continues to attack God's purpose and design and has directly confronted, contradicted, and distorted God's word through compromise and justification. The consequences of entertaining his twisted thinking have been lost fellowship with God, eviction from the Garden of Eden, and the curse of sickness, poverty, and death. Had it not been for God's mercy, we would have all had to add eternal separation and darkness to the list. However, despite the substantial cost of rebellion, Satan draws away millions of people using the same tactics; the lust of the flesh, the lust of the eyes, and the pride of life. The infamous words spoken by the serpent to Eve in the Garden of Eden "For God doth know that in the day ye eat thereof your eyes shall be opened, and ye shall be as gods, knowing good and evil," have become permanently imprinted in man's DNA. It is a virus which lies dormant in the darkest parts of our minds waiting for an opportunity to resurface and wield its influence. The thought of being the center of the universe, being as God as opposed to being subject to God, and the freedom to do as thou wilt continues to be a spiritual parasite in the lives of many. The result is vain imaginations and a foolish, darkened heart. Christians are not exempt from this deception, and the more we get away from sound doctrine, the more foolish our hearts become. As I stated earlier, you never lose the right to choose, and your choices can lead to deception even after you receive Jesus Christ.

<u>Romans 1:21-22</u>
1:21 "Because that, when they knew God, they glorified him not as God, neither were thankful; but became vain in their imaginations, and their foolish heart was darkened."
1:22 "Professing themselves to be wise, they became fools,"

Another deception is we live in a society that calls good evil and evil good, to justify man's choice to live outside of God's will, purpose, and design. Even in the face of the Bible warning us these days would come, this thinking is embraced like a virus in the souls of the masses who are so willing to be infected. Those who advocate for God's design are vilified and silenced for the audacity to promote such archaic Biblical beliefs. They contend, how dare you promote marriage between a man and a woman in the face of anatomy, you hateful and treacherous being? How dare you say a boy is a boy, and a girl is a girl when the truth is so apparent by looking at them you shameless bully? How dare you say a fetus is alive when it so small? How dare you say the sexualization of our youth is harmful when doing so infringes on their rights and self-expression? Or promote the idea safeguards should be put in place to filter what they see and hear you out of touch Neanderthal? They contend it should be apparent promoting the Bible is an evil worthy of the most extreme punishment. Mere mumblings of wicked fundamentalist, who seek to infect the world with hate and destroy the environment and should be outlawed and banned from the public sphere. All while immorality is encouraged and celebrated, rebellion is fashionable and praised, murder is justified, and from an early age the eyes of the innocent are not spared as families destroyed and lust spread like a plague. Despite the blatant disregard for common sense, the more these ideas are backed, promoted, and endorsed by the media, celebrities, and the social media mafia, the more brainwashed society becomes. We are bombarded daily with countless images designed to reinforce the new narrative anything less than acceptance is hate. To disagree is to hate when it used to be a disagreement. So now you see the collision course we are on you either abandon the Bible or become an enemy of the State.

To see the devastating results of this thinking look at the impact on the black community, my community, where so many fathers are not in the home, and we drift further and further away from the Word of God. The many young black girls who lack a covering which protects them from negative influences and builds up and guards their self-esteem. The young boys who are in search of an identity and so desperately need the guidance, discipline, and direction only a strong father can bring. There was a time in our community where families were strong, the church was the center of our community, and there was a big Bible on every living room table. Just seeing the Bible meant something regardless as to the spiritual condition of the home. It was a starting point symbolizing the strength of the Black community in the face of impossible odds. We gave God thanks for bringing us through tough and challenging times. It was our faith in Him that kept us strong and bonded our community together. It reminded us of our will and determination, which enabled us to overcome the racism and discrimination we faced. We had respect for our elders and were quick to straighten up when one walked in the room. Some had parents, others grandmothers, who taught them the Word, took them to church, and showed us values, morals, and respect. Many times we felt as if we only had each other and were so happy when another black person walked in the room. In looking at the madness of the world around us we would jokingly say things like "I know a black person didn't do that" because there were certain things, we felt we did not do. Now in the face of progress and living the American dream, we have all but forgotten and abandoned the God we once served and loved and not only will we "do that," in some ways we do worst. We are painfully discovering you can't just throw the Bible out without throwing out the countless jewels, wisdom, and values it contains. The aftermath of worldly success has left us as sheep without a shepherd being led away from righteousness and truth. We have all but forgotten it wasn't too long ago when all we had was God. One needs only ask as we drift further away from the Bible are things getting better or worse?

<u>Isaiah 5:20</u> "Woe unto them that call evil good, and good evil; that put darkness for light, and light for darkness; that put bitter for sweet, and sweet for bitter!"

Through our churches, heavy Christian influence, the availability of the gospel, and free exercise of religion, we have prospered as a nation and in the world around us. We are now witnessing severe signs of deterioration, the weakening of the church, and compromised lifestyles of professing Christians as we continue to gain momentum on this downward spiral. It is a meticulous plan of spiritual erosion accelerated by infiltrating the very heart of our Christian faith, the church.

Isaiah 9:16 "For the leaders of this people cause them to err; and they that are led of them are destroyed."

HOW TO OVERCOME DECEPTION:

I Thessalonians 5:5-6
5:5 "Ye are all the children of light, and the children of the day: we are not of the night, nor of darkness."
5:6 "Therefore let us not sleep, as *do* others; but let us watch and be sober."

The Lord never intended for His church to be deceived and has given us a proven defense against all darkness. It is tried and true, has never been compromised, and withstood the test of time. It is an infallible source of wisdom that will never let us down, has an answer for every problem and challenge we face, and proven to be more reliable than any other information known to man. This fantastic and phenomenal source is the Bible, the unadulterated Word of God. It is a supernatural book that both lives and

194

breathes — fueled by the faith of those who have accepted and believe in the Lord Jesus Christ.

Biblical faith is the straight and narrow bridge which carries the mind beyond the confines and limitations of reality to the supernatural understanding of a God you cannot see or touch. Because our minds are incapable of processing spiritual things, God gave us faith to bridge the gap between the natural and supernatural. It has no curves or deviation thus the Bible is either 100% true or 100% wrong because only pure unadulterated faith transforms the Bible from an interesting piece of literature to the very life and essence of God.

II Timothy 3:16-17
3:16 "All scripture [is] given by inspiration of God, and [is] profitable for doctrine, for reproof, for correction, for instruction in righteousness:
3:17 "That the man of God may be perfect, throughly furnished unto all good works."

II Peter 1:20-21
1:20 "Knowing this first, that no prophecy of the scripture is of any private interpretation."
1:21 "For the prophecy came not in old time by the will of man: but holy men of God spake [as they were] moved by the Holy Ghost."

Revelation 22:18-19
22:18 "For I testify unto every man that heareth the words of the prophecy of this book, If any man shall add unto these things, God shall add unto him the plagues that are written in this book:"
22:19 "And if any man shall take away from the words of the book of this prophecy, God shall take away his part out of the book of life, and out of the holy city, and [from] the things which are written in this book."

Hebrews 4:12 "For the word of God [is] quick, and powerful, and sharper than any twoedged sword, piercing even to the dividing asunder of soul and spirit, and of the joints and marrow, and [is] a discerner of the thoughts and intents of the heart."

Matthew 7:13-14
7:13 "Enter ye in at the strait gate: for wide *is* the gate, and broad *is* the way, that leadeth to destruction, and many there be which go in thereat:"
7:14 "Because strait *is* the gate, and narrow *is* the way, which leadeth unto life, and few there be that find it.

I Corinthians 2:12-14
2:12 "Now we have received, not the spirit of the world, but the spirit which is of God; that we might know the things that are freely given to us of God."
2:13 "Which things also we speak, not in the words which man's wisdom teacheth, but which the Holy Ghost teacheth; comparing spiritual things with spiritual."
2:14 "But the natural man receiveth not the things of the Spirit of God: for they are foolishness unto him:

196

neither can he know *them*, because they are spiritually discerned."

God has also given us His Spirit to overcome the days we in which we live. The Bible tells us He will teach us all things, bring things to our remembrance, convict us of sin, and warn us when danger approaches. The Holy Ghost, also called the Spirit of Truth, the Holy Spirit, and the Comforter is the third member of the Trinity. He has many functions such as intercession on our behalf and the behalf of others, praying out the will and mysteries of God into the earth, comforting the body of Christ, reproving the world of sin, righteousness, and judgment, guiding and directing us into all truth. He bears witness of the Lord Jesus Christ. He provides us revelation and understanding and manifests the power of God in our lives including boldness, miracles, signs and wonders, manifestation of the fruits of the Spirit, healings, and other demonstrations of the power of God.

Every believer must know what the word says concerning the Holy Ghost and accept this precious gift God made available. The discussion should not be based on opinion or denominational doctrines, but faith and belief in what the Word says. A lack of faith is the main reason people fall short when it comes to the manifestation of God's power in their lives. You must take God at His Word and have the faith to believe what He says.

Romans 8:14 "For as many as are led by the Spirit of God, they are the sons of God"

John 16:7-11
16:7 "Nevertheless I tell you the truth; It is expedient for you that I go away: for if I go not away, the Comforter will not come unto you; but if I depart, I will send Him unto you."
16:8 "And when He comes, He will reprove the world of sin, and of righteousness, and of judgment:"
16:9 "Of sin, because they believe not on me;"
16:10 "Of righteousness, because I go to my Father, and ye see me no more;"
16:11 "Of judgment, because the prince of this world is judged."

I John 2:27 "But the anointing which ye have received of Him abideth in you, and ye need not that any man teach you: but as the same anointing teacheth you of all things, and is truth, and is no lie, and even as it hath taught you, ye shall abide in Him."

John 16:13-14
16:13 "Howbeit when he, the Spirit of Truth, is come, he will guide you into all truth: for he shall not speak of himself; but whatsoever he shall hear, that shall he speak: and will shew you things to come."
16:14 "He shall glorify me: for he shall receive of mine, and shall shew it unto you."

John 14:26 "But the comforter, which is the Holy Ghost, whom the father will send in my name, He shall teach you all things, and bring all things to your remembrance, whatsoever I have said unto you."

Luke 12:12 "For the Holy Ghost will teach you in that same hour what ye ought to say"

Acts 2:1-4
2:1 "And when the day of Pentecost was fully come, they were all with one accord in one place."
2:2 "And suddenly there came a sound from heaven as of a rushing mighty wind, and it filled all the house where they were sitting."
2:3 "And there appeared unto them cloven tongues like as of fire, and it sat upon each of them."
2:4 "And they were all filled with the Holy Ghost, and began to speak with other tongues, as the Spirit gave them utterance."

During these times, we must receive clear and concise directions from the Lord. We have all the tools we need to overcome the deceptions of Satan, but it is

199

up to us to take advantage of them. The Bible says, "my people are destroyed for lack of knowledge," and refusing to spend time with God through reading His word and prayer will thrust you headlong into that category of defeated saints. God will never take away your right to choose whether to be in fellowship with him. Satan's deception can cause you to deny the Lord Jesus Christ by reducing Him to that of a good man, as opposed to the absolute Saviour. It can lead to an ungodly and unrepented lifestyle by viewing the Bible as a reference point and not the final authority of God. In the days ahead, it may even result in you giving your allegiance to a satanic system of government characterized by receiving the mark of the beast.

Philippians 2:12 "Wherefore, my beloved, as ye have always obeyed, not as in my presence only, but now much more in my absence, work out your salvation with fear and trembling."

II. Timothy 2:15-16
2:15 "Study to shew thyself approved unto God, a workman that needeth not to be ashamed, rightly dividing the word of truth."
2:16 "But shun profane and vain babblings: for they will increase unto more ungodliness."

Proverbs 14:12 "There is a way which seemeth right unto a man, but the end thereof are the ways of death."

Prayer Apostasy

Eternal Father, True and Living God, who is the Beginning and the End. We come before you, in the name of Jesus, declaring you are the God of the Heavens above and the Earth beneath and all things are in your grasp and subject to your reach. You are in complete control and even the depths of the earth answer to your voice. In the name of Jesus and the power of His Blood, we come against the spirit of apostasy that causes men to turn away from the faith and revelation of truth contained in your word. We come against and destroy every evil influence and rebellious thoughts that lead men into disobedience. In the name of Jesus, we demolish false religious spirits, ideologies, and doctrines of demons seeking to distort the truth of God's sovereign design and plan, and rebuke all doubt and disbelief leading to deceit and spiritual darkness. Let men heed to sound doctrine, inspired by the very breath of God, and not be led astray by their lust and carnal desires. In the name of Jesus and the power of His Blood, we bind the devices of Satan that blind the hearts and minds of those who do not believe and pray for revival and spiritual awakening to rise in the land. That men repent of their evil ways and backsliding and turn back to you. In the name of Jesus, please cleanse our hearts, so they are not wicked and unbelieving and let us remain faithful until the very end. Help us to endure hardship and offense and not be deterred by fear and persecution. We trust in you, Lord, and place our lives in your hands. We stand on your word that declares we are always in your thoughts and your plans for us are good and not evil. You have provided us a future filled with hope and the peace that comes from resting in you. In Jesus name, we pray, Thank God – Amen.

Judgment

A GENERATION THAT KNOWS NOT GOD OR HIS WORKS

Many years ago, the Lord revealed to me a prophetic vision of the days to come. As I lay in my bed, it was as if the Lord carried me away and put me in the middle of a school playground. It reminded me of recess or lunchtime. It appeared to be a perfectly normal day, and there were hundreds of youth ranging in age, laughing, playing and running around. At first, it seemed very innocent, but as I stood there, the scene began to change quickly as I noticed the children engaging in all sorts of deviant and sexual behavior. As I watched, the laughter grew louder and became more like a celebration or ritual of defiance openly drinking alcohol, using drugs, and engaging in very lewd and lascivious behavior for all to see. Even though they knew I was standing there, at times looking each other right in the face, the children had no shame or inhibitions as they taunted me with their ungodly behavior and brazen debauchery. Despite the

204

outrageous and immoral acts being committed, they appeared to be totally at ease and unrestrained. As I continued to observe, I heard multiple gunshots, and they began to fall one upon another as they were hit by the random bullets piercing the air. The laughter turned to screaming as they fell to the ground ducking for cover like they were used to this drill. Moments later when the shooting stopped, they quickly jumped up as if nothing had happened, merely stepping over the dead bodies which had blood pouring out of them. The laughter and playing started again, and the children returned to using drugs and participating in the demonic orgy despite the many dead bodies fresh on the ground. The Lord then spoke to me and said there would come a lost generation that will not repent and turn from their wicked ways. He told me to pray. The Lord then led me to the following scriptures in the book of Judges.

Judges 2:8-14
2:8 "And Joshua the son of Nun, the servant of the LORD, died, *being* an hundred and ten years old."
2:9 "And they buried him in the border of his inheritance in Timnathheres, in the mount of Ephraim, on the north side of the hill Gaash."
2:10 "And also all that generation were gathered unto their fathers: and there arose another generation after

them, which knew not the LORD, nor yet the works which he had done for Israel."

2:11 "And the children of Israel did evil in the sight of the LORD, and served Baalim:"

2:12 "And they forsook the LORD God of their fathers, which brought them out of the land of Egypt, and followed other gods, of the gods of the people that *were* round about them, and bowed themselves unto them, and provoked the LORD to anger."

2:13 "And they forsook the LORD, and served Baal and Ashtaroth."

2:14 "And the anger of the LORD was hot against Israel, and he delivered them into the hands of spoilers that spoiled them, and he sold them into the hands of their enemies round about, so that they could not any longer stand before their enemies."

The generation described arose after Joshua's generation had grown old and died. It was Joshua who succeeded Moses in whom the Lord used to deliver the children of Israel out of bondage when they cried out to Him while captive in Egypt. It was through Moses the Lord performed great miracles in the eyes of Pharaoh, including parting the Red Sea and devouring the massive Egyptian army which pursued behind them with their mighty horsemen and chariots. It was Moses who led them into the wilderness where the Lord tried and proved them so they would know He was their

God. After years of murmuring, doubt, and unbelief it was Joshua, who succeeded Moses and led their children into the promised land. The Lord fought their battles, and they conquered great nations to come into their inheritance. Throughout their tribes, they were taught the stories of their forefathers Abraham, Isaac, and Jacob and rehearsed the faithfulness God had shown them because they walked in covenant with Him. They rehearsed the statues and commandments of God, and even the hardness of their fathers' hearts, and passed down these teachings from generation to generation. Even in the days preceding his passing, Joshua once again reminded the people not to forsake the Almighty God by turning away from His statutes and commandments and serving other gods. Just as Satan referred to as the god of this world, these false gods represented the abominations in the land and the foolishness of men, who created idols made with hands, while refusing to honor and give thanks to the True and Living God who created all things.

Joshua 24:20-25

24:20 "If ye forsake the LORD, and serve strange gods, then he will turn and do you hurt, and consume you, after that he hath done you good."

24:21 "And the people said unto Joshua, Nay; but we will serve the LORD."

24:22 "And Joshua said unto the people, Ye *are* witnesses against yourselves that ye have chosen you the LORD, to serve him. And they said, *We are* witnesses."

24:23 "Now therefore put away, *said he*, the strange gods which *are* among you, and incline your heart unto the LORD God of Israel."

24:24 "And the people said unto Joshua, The LORD our God will we serve, and his voice will we obey."

After Joshua passed, there arose another generation that did not take heed to obey God's instructions and began to make covenants with the people in the land round about them. They abandoned the God of their fathers and forsook the warnings that had been passed down from generations. They committed great evil and abominations in His sight and did not rehearse the great works He had performed on their behalf in the ears of their children. As a result, they did not acknowledge or fear the Lord. They did not know His ways, nor did they regard His statutes and commandments. They provoked God to great anger and wrath, and He told them He would no longer drive out their enemies from before them, and they would become thorns in their sides, and their gods would be a snare unto them. It was a lost generation who worshiped idols and false gods, even sacrificing their children to the gods in the land. The Lord burned with anger against them so that they could no longer withstand their enemies and He handed them over to people who plundered and destroyed them.

Judges 2:15 "Whithersoever they went out, the hand of the LORD was against them for evil, as the LORD had said, and as the LORD had sworn unto them: and they were greatly distressed."

It is important to note, a generation, as described earlier, refers to the collective consciousness of a group of people living during the same time. Throughout the Bible, there were times when the nation of Israel collectively acknowledged the Lord and did those things that were pleasing in His sight and other times when they rebelled against Him. There were times when holiness prevailed and times when they were consumed with evil and wickedness. Despite the various states, Israel found itself in; God always has a remnant in every generation that will repent and turn back to Him. Even in a lost generation, there are those who love the Lord, those won to the Lord, and those in whom the Lord will touch their hearts and draw them back to Him. We are called to pray for all men with the hope they will come into the knowledge of the truth, but in a lost generation, there is a drastic shift in the collective consciousness and the direction of the spiritual current turned against God. When nations turn against God, His judgment and wrath always follow. The Lord is longsuffering and gives men space to repent, but He is a Holy God that avenges all unrighteousness and sin.

"A generation that knew not God nor His works."

The generation the Lord showed me in the vision, is the type of society we are witnessing today where we are trending away from God. A generation greatly distressed because they are operating outside of the will of God, His statutes and commandments. They lack peace, are unsteady, restless, and confused in their thinking and behavior. A prideful generation without a God consciousness, having no defined spiritual direction, in which many people are confused and struggling to find their true identity. Because the Lord Almighty is in direct opposition with the things of this world, the more they pursue and cling to carnal things, the more they despise the God who seemingly stands in their way. Despite the visible signs of societal breakdown such as depression, hopelessness, anxiety, high suicide rates, dysfunctional homes, and a lack of contentment, they march deeper into the darkness with no end in sight.

Proverbs 30:11-14
30:11 *"There is* a generation *that* curseth their father, and doth not bless their mother."
30:12 *"There is* a generation *that are* pure in their own eyes, and *yet* is not washed from their filthiness"
30:13 *"There is* a generation, O how lofty are their eyes! and their eyelids are lifted up."
30:14 *"There is* a generation, whose teeth *are as* swords, and their jaw teeth *as* knives, to devour the poor from off the earth, and the needy from *among* men."

John 3:19-20
3:19 "And this is the condemnation, that light is come into the world, and men loved darkness rather than light, because their deeds were evil."

3:20 "For every one that doeth evil hateth the light, neither cometh to the light, lest his deeds should be reproved."

This generation does not acknowledge God, nor do they know His ways. They do not remember His faithfulness and how He gave His Only Begotten Son to redeem us from our fallen nature and cleanse us from our sins. His hand has been upon our nation for good, and He has protected and prospered our way. There are countless testimonies of healings and deliverance, and many difficult and challenging times He has brought us through. How when other nations were experiencing wars on their soil and famine in their land, He made us a beacon of light and hope for all the world to see just as He did for Israel when they walked in covenant with Him. Despite His great works, a generation has emerged that has no reverence or fear of God, openly mocking Him and blaspheming His name, and showing no regard for His ways. A generation indoctrinated through social engineering resulting in a hive mentality influenced by social media, Hollywood celebrities and lifestyles, pop culture and fashion, the music and film industry, arts and entertainment, educational institutions, humanism, and other influences which guide the development and behavior of society. These norms are reinforced and affirmed, keeping them in line with the collective consciousness pushed. Each day they are bombarded with thousands of ungodly and sexual images designed to keep them in a state of self-will and rebellion. It is a generation built on having fun as if the party will never end, as if there is no accountability or a price to pay for their sins, and fueled by the perception even when life ceases their self-determined notions of morality and goodness will lead them to a better place.

Satan's agenda of erasing the God-consciousness is evident in this generation. There are no moral absolutes and anything, and everything goes. In other words, "do as thou wilt" is fully embraced by this generation. It is a belief system which seeks to liberate man from his consciousness of God by indulging the flesh, where the Bible says to crucify it. Indulging the flesh is like biting the forbidden fruit, and the more we partake of the apple of illumination, our minds are freed from the restrictions placed on us by

God. They embrace this ideology as the path to enlightenment, and the more the flesh defiled, the more their spirits are set free, not understanding the unintended consequences of opening Pandora's box. The more they entertain darkness and depravity, the more they satisfy their deepest sexual fantasies and perversions, the more bombarded with satanic and occult symbolism, the more they deface and defile their bodies and the more they celebrate sin, they are released from captivity and free to receive and live in the gnosis they are as gods. The result is satanism has become mainstream by bringing what was once taboo to the forefront of society. The more exposed, the more accepting we are without understanding these ungodly symbols convey meaning, dark power, and spiritual significance. They have no idea this is by design to make them ripe for satanic influence and initiation into the occult.

It is a generation that lacks conviction because they have been taught to embrace their fallen nature as opposed to being delivered from it; thus, it appears to many young people Christians hate everything they love. They feel we are attacking their loved ones, friends, and even them because they are different or have challenges in their lives. The result is resentment and anger towards God, a loss of faith in the values that once shaped our society, seeing good as evil and evil as good, a lack of respect for parents and family, and moral breakdown. They misconstrue the idea of love and weaponize concepts such as diversity, tolerance, and inclusion because they do not know what submission to God means or the basis for even doing it. The result is a society with no restraints, no regrets, no remorse, and no repentance. The very definition of the word inclusive implies it is a door that can never be shut and we must be willing to accept whatever walks in. This is driven by the premise man is inherently good and his heart will produce good things. Yet the Bible says we are born in sin and shapen in iniquity.

God consciousness

Galatians 5:22-25
5:22 "But the fruit of the Spirit is love, joy, peace, longsuffering, gentleness, goodness, faith,"
5:23 "Meekness, temperance: against such, there is no law."

215

5:24 "And they that are Christ's have crucified the flesh with the affections and lusts."
5:25 "If we live in the Spirit, let us also walk in the Spirit."

The consciousness of this world

Galatians 5:19-21
5:19 "Now the works of the flesh are manifest, which are *these*; Adultery, fornication, uncleanness, lasciviousness,"
5:20 "Idolatry, witchcraft, hatred, variance, emulations, wrath, strife, seditions, heresies,"
5:21 "Envyings, murders, drunkenness, revellings, and such like: of the which I tell you before, as I have also told *you* in time past, that they which do such things shall not inherit the kingdom of God."

Just as the generation in the Book of Judges went after idols and strange gods, this generation has gone after the same. Modern-day idolatry is fueled by the lust for the materialism and vices of this world. It can include putting money before morality, chasing after the ungodly lifestyles of those who promote the things of this world and selling one's soul or allegiance to Satan for worldly success. Many young people imitate celebrities without much thought. They no longer worship idols made from hands such as wood

216

and stone but have made idols of men and women who have sold their souls for worldly fame. Many celebrities appear to be larger than life and worshiped by their fans and followers, but there is a price to pay for worldly fame which is why they speak from the same script and promote the same things. What many young people don't understand is their fame and success depends on pushing the agendas of those who sign their checks, and even a slight deviation from the norm will cost them everything. I am not saying every celebrity is corrupt, but the system they operate in is. There are those who do it willingly and others because they feel they have no choice, but the result is the same. How many celebrities are willing to boldly say they believe the Bible and teachings of Jesus Christ and are willing to face the backlash? How many will say they stand for marriage between a man and a woman, or support the right to life, or will say Jesus Christ is the only way? Even those who profess to be Christian act and look the same as those who say they are not. It is because they are part of a system that defines what they can say, what causes they must represent, the symbols they must use, what they can and cannot promote, and that system is becoming darker and darker. Across the board, in every major industry where you see celebrities, entertainers, and people in the spotlight, you are seeing the same satanic symbols and hear the same scripted views, none of which support anything Biblical. These are the people this generation looks to for guidance and direction.

No restraints, no remorse, no regrets.

II Timothy 3:1-5
3:1 "This know also, that in the last days perilous times shall come."
3:2 "For men shall be lovers of their own selves, covetous, boasters, proud, blasphemers, disobedient to parents, unthankful, unholy,"
3:3 "Without natural affection, trucebreakers, false accusers, incontinent, fierce, despisers of those that are good,"
3:4 "Traitors, heady, highminded, lovers of pleasures more than lovers of God;"
3:5 "Having a form of godliness, but denying the power thereof: from such turn away."

Luke 4:5-7
4:5 "And the devil, taking him up into an high mountain, shewed unto him all the kingdoms of the world in a moment of time."

218

4:6 "And the devil said unto him, All this power will I give thee, and the glory of them: for that is delivered unto me; and to whomsoever I will I give it.

I Timothy 6:10-11
6:10 "For the love of money is the root of all evil: which while some coveted after, they have erred from the faith, and pierced themselves through with many sorrows."
6:11 "But thou, O man of God, flee these things; and follow after righteousness, godliness, faith, love, patience, meekness."

A lost generation doesn't understand we are born into this world under the influence of Satan. They have no concept of a fallen nature or the need to be born again by accepting Jesus Christ. They have not been taught about God or His ways and have no gatekeepers to shield them from the deception of this world. The way God intended for generations to thrive was through the family, but it is under constant attack and, in many cases, destroyed. The purpose of the family was to model the design and purpose of God, passing His statutes and commandments down from generation to generation so our children would know His ways and experience His great love. It is the vehicle God uses to shield them from the immorality and

219

deception of this world and protect their innocence from an adversary who seeks to devour them. It is the first line of defense designed to safeguard the hearts and minds of children by providing them guidance and correction and reminding them of the judgment of God. The place where young people develop an identity rooted in the teachings of Christ as opposed to the influence of this scripted world. In the absence of the family to instruct children in righteousness, many are preyed upon and left without a fighting chance. God chose Abraham to be the Father of Nations because He saw in his heart that he would faithfully teach his children to walk in all His ways.

Genesis 18:19 "For I know him, that he will command his children and his household after him, and they shall keep the way of the LORD, to do justice and judgment; that the LORD may bring upon Abraham that which he hath spoken of him."

Deuteronomy 6:4-14
6:4 "Hear, O Israel: The LORD our God *is* one LORD:"
6:5 "And thou shalt love the LORD thy God with all thine heart, and with all thy soul, and with all thy might."
6:6 "And these words, which I command thee this day, shall be in thine heart:"

6:7 "And thou shalt teach them diligently unto thy children, and shalt talk of them when thou sittest in thine house, and when thou walkest by the way, and when thou liest down, and when thou risest up."
6:8 "And thou shalt bind them for a sign upon thine hand, and they shall be as frontlets between thine eyes."
6:9 "And thou shalt write them upon the posts of thy house, and on thy gates."
6:10 "And it shall be, when the LORD thy God shall have brought thee into the land which he sware unto thy fathers, to Abraham, to Isaac, and to Jacob, to give thee great and goodly cities, which thou buildedst not,"
6:11 "And houses full of all good *things*, which thou filledst not, and wells digged, which thou diggedst not, vineyards and olive trees, which thou plantedst not; when thou shalt have eaten and be full;"
6:12 "*Then* beware lest thou forget the LORD, which brought thee forth out of the land of Egypt, from the house of bondage."
6:13 "Thou shalt fear the LORD thy God, and serve him, and shalt swear by his name."
6:14 "Ye shall not go after other gods, of the gods of the people which *are* round about you;"

Proverbs 22:6 "Train up a child in the way he should go: and when he is old, he will not depart from it."

Satan's goal is the destruction of the family because, in the absence of the family, people will look to the world for identity and guidance. The young because they have not been taught the ways of the Lord and the old because they have forgotten. Satan is the god of this world and exercises power and authority over it. Since the fall of man, the world has lived in rebellion to God. There is nothing new under the sun when it comes to lust and pride only the magnitude in which it flourishes and manifests itself. In other words, the world continues to do what the world has always done. Things are getting drastically worst because the light that was put in the earth to restrain the darkness is starting to fade. Many people are deceived into believing they must agree with Satan's plans when all that's required is; they live according to it. In a previous chapter, we saw when Nimrod built the Tower of Babel; the masses weren't included in the planning they merely supplied the labor and the bricks. Meaning they did not have to be aware of the agenda to be used to carry it out. This generation will supply the bricks and foundation upon which the New World Order /Tower of Babel will be built. In the absence of God, the stage has been set for the emergence of the anti-christ, and we see the great falling away from Lord the Bible warned us would come. We see the formation of a society that no longer has God at its center and celebrates darkness. A society where "Do as thou Wilt," is the whole of the law.

II Thessalonians 2:3 "Let no man deceive you by any means: for *that day shall not come*, except there come a falling away first, and that man of sin be revealed, the son of perdition;"

Matthew 24:13 "But he that shall endure unto the end, the same shall be saved."

TIME OF JUDGMENT

TO ENDURE UNTIL THE END, WE MUST UNDERSTAND WHAT THE BIBLE SAYS CONCERNING JUDGMENT

As a nation, we no longer fear God and have turned away from serving Him. We no longer honor His institutions, we have left from following His statutes and commandments, we sacrifice the innocent and no longer preserve the sanctity of marriage, family, and life. We call evil good and good evil, we no longer acknowledge Him or give Him thanks, we have given over to seducing spirits and doctrines of demons, and we openly embrace the occult and satanic symbolism.

We neglect the cry of the poor, we are rebellious and prideful, and our hearts have become hardened with sin. We mock Christian morals and values and drive Biblical principles out of our institutions and the public sphere.

Despite how egregious these offenses may sound, they are circumstances common to man and many nations and societies before us have fallen out of fellowship with God. As stated earlier, the nation of Israel would fall in and out of fellowship with God, even going after false gods, sacrificing their children to Baal and committing great evil and wickedness in His sight. God always received them back when they humbled themselves, sought His face and repented for their sins. God has an answer for sin, and His mercies are new every morning. Great is God's faithfulness, and His love is beyond understanding.

II Chronicles 7:13-15
7:13 "If I shut up heaven that there be no rain, or if I command the locusts to devour the land, or if I send pestilence among my people;"
7:14 "If my people, which are called by my name, shall humble themselves, and pray, and seek my face, and turn from their wicked ways; then will I hear from

224

heaven, and will forgive their sin, and will heal their land."
7:15 "Now mine eyes shall be open, and mine ears attent unto the prayer *that is made* in this place."

Lamentations 3:22-23
3:22 "*It is of* the LORD'S mercies that we are not consumed, because his compassions fail not."
3:23 "*They are* new every morning: great *is* thy faithfulness."

Sin is not the reason why this nation will experience the wrath of God; it is because the very fabric of this nation has changed, and it refuses to repent. In other words, America is on a collision course with God's wrath, because it has ignored His cries for repentance and has become prideful and arrogant and is entering a state of total rebellion. America has never been a perfect nation, but it was a nation with many people who feared and honored God, and its laws and institutions were set up based on Biblical principles and values. America has not always practiced what it preached, has not been immune from Satan's power and influence, and there have been hidden agendas, but it was this nation God chose to send evangelist all over the world, spreading the good news of Jesus Christ. It has also been blessed because of its favorable treatment of the Nation of Israel.

Genesis 12:1-3
12:1 "Now the LORD had said unto Abram, Get thee out of thy country, and from thy kindred, and from thy father's house, unto a land that I will shew thee:"
12:2 "And I will make of thee a great nation, and I will bless thee, and make thy name great; and thou shalt be a blessing:"
12:3 "And I will bless them that bless thee, and curse him that curseth thee: and in thee shall all families of the earth be blessed."

Viewed in the eyes of the world as a Christian nation, powerful voices like the Reverend Billy Graham could be heard in revivals across the country spreading the gospel, and millions of people received the Lord Jesus Christ. There were strong churches, and children taught — biblical values and morality. Yes, God used a nation of imperfect people, some full of hatred and greed, to accomplish His purpose in the earth despite its shortcomings and weaknesses. Within America, there was still light in the heart's of the faithful, shining amid the darkness, drawing wicked and sinful men to repentance. Many people who have traveled around the world often say how fortunate even the poorest

Americans are considering what they have seen. God is a God of covenant, and in the past America has walked in covenant with God, and He has blessed our nation. For this reason alone, I would never burn a flag, because despite our weaknesses, I am so grateful for what God has done for this nation.

Now there is a shift that has not only affected the nation but the church as well. The Bible warns us a divided nation cannot stand, and America is more divided now than it has ever been. It has left its foundation and roots and embarked down a dark path of no return. The common thread that held us together was our belief and fear of God. As a nation, we cried out to the God of the Bible for protection, strength, and guidance. We had respect for the church and leaders were held in high esteem. Whenever we faced adversity, we prayed and acknowledged God in the eyes of the world and looked to the church for spiritual direction. Now we are pushing God out of every corner of society at an accelerated pace and silencing the one voice that could lead us to repentance. We are even making laws aimed to restrict the rights of parents to raise their children based on biblical values and are dangerously close to criminalizing parts of the Bible and imposing fines and imprisonment on those who advocate its teachings. America is becoming a society tolerant of everything except a Christian's right to honor and obey the God they love. Christian ideas and principles are mocked and attacked regularly, and we no longer want to be recognized as a Christian nation. In the absence of repentance, we are subject to the same fate as other nations who turned their back on God. In His wrath, He will take His hands off this nation, leaving us to fight our battles and to solve our problems. America will be turned over to the very dark spirits it embraces, and our enemies will become a snare unto us. This proud nation that relies on its military strength and wealth will discover as other great empires have it is God that raises one up and sits down another. It is God who has all power and authority and repays those that hate Him to their face.

Matthew 12:25 "And Jesus knew their thoughts, and said unto them, Every kingdom divided against itself is brought to desolation; and every city or house divided against itself shall not stand:"

Revelation 18:1-8

18:1 "And after these things I saw another angel come down from heaven, having great power; and the earth was lightened with his glory."

18:2 "And he cried mightily with a strong voice, saying, Babylon the great is fallen, is fallen, and is become the habitation of devils, and the hold of every foul spirit, and a cage of every unclean and hateful bird."

18:3 "For all nations have drunk of the wine of the wrath of her fornication, and the kings of the earth have committed fornication with her, and the merchants of the earth are waxed rich through the abundance of her delicacies."

18:4 "And I heard another voice from heaven, saying, Come out of her, my people, that ye be not partakers of her sins, and that ye receive not of her plagues."

18:5 "For her sins have reached unto heaven, and God hath remembered her iniquities."

18:6 "Reward her even as she rewarded you, and double unto her double according to her works: in the cup which she hath filled fill to her double."

18:7 "How much she hath glorified herself, and lived deliciously, so much torment and sorrow give her: for she saith in her heart, I sit a queen, and am no widow, and shall see no sorrow."

18:8 "Therefore shall her plagues come in one day, death, and mourning, and famine; and she shall be utterly burned with fire: for strong *is* the Lord God who judgeth her."

18:9 "And the kings of the earth, who have committed fornication and lived deliciously with her, shall bewail

229

her, and lament for her, when they shall see the smoke of her burning,"
18:10 "Standing afar off for the fear of her torment, saying, Alas, alas, that great city Babylon, that mighty city! for in one hour is thy judgment come."

There will be those who deny the judgment of God and will continue to prophesy and promise the people great things. They will keep chasing the material things of this world speaking of peace and days of ease. They will not warn the body of the days to come, nor will they prepare the hearts of the people to be judged. Do not put your faith in these men and trust what the Word of God says concerning these days.

Jeremiah 23:16-17; 21-22
23:16 "Thus saith the LORD of hosts, Hearken not unto the words of the prophets that prophesy unto you: they make you vain: they speak a vision of their own heart, and not out of the mouth of the LORD."
23:17 "They say still unto them that despise me, The LORD hath said, Ye shall have peace; and they say unto every one that walketh after the imagination of his own heart, No evil shall come upon you."
23:21 "I have not sent these prophets, yet they ran: I have not spoken to them, yet they prophesied."
23:22 "But if they had stood in my counsel, and had caused my people to hear my words, then they should have turned them from their evil way, and from the evil of their doings."

Luke 12:54-57

12:54 "And he said also to the people, When ye see a cloud rise out of the west, straightway ye say, There cometh a shower; and so it is."

12:55 "And when *ye see* the south wind blow, ye say, There will be heat; and it cometh to pass."

12:56 "*Ye* hypocrites, ye can discern the face of the sky and of the earth; but how is it that ye do not discern this time?"

12:57 "Yea, and why even of yourselves judge ye not what is right?"

God does not Judge the Righteous with the Wicked.

The first thing to consider concerning the Judgment of God is He does not judge the righteous with the wicked. The church is judged based on the mercy, love, and faithfulness of God for purification. The world is judged based on the wrath of God to punish it for its sin. Note, in the following scriptures, Noah and his family were not judged the same way the world was judged and did not experience the wrath of God. He had faith in God's warnings and adequately prepared when the wrath of God was poured out upon the earth. The hope we have in this time of judgment is the Bible says when the Lord returns it shall be just as it was in the days of Noah. Just as in the days of Noah,

231

the wickedness of men is great in the earth, and the thoughts of his heart are evil. There is continuous sin and iniquity, and the wrath of the Lord will be poured out upon the earth, but there is hope for the believer. The Bible warns us of the wrath to come, and those who have faith in God's Word can be adequately prepared to find safety in the ark and escape God's wrath. The Bible says God will keep His people out of the hour of testing or tribulation period that is to come upon the earth. This event will not be a physical ark, rather; the rapture of the church or being caught up to be with the Lord.

Genesis 6:5-8
6:5 "And GOD saw that the wickedness of man *was* great in the earth, and *that* every imagination of the thoughts of his heart *was* only evil continually."
6:6 "And it repented the LORD that he had made man on the earth, and it grieved him at his heart."
6:7 "And the LORD said, I will destroy man whom I have created from the face of the earth; both man, and beast, and the creeping thing, and the fowls of the air; for it repenteth me that I have made them."
6:8 "But Noah found grace in the eyes of the LORD."

Matthew 24:37 "But as the days of Noe *were*, so shall also the coming of the Son of man be."

II Peter 2:9 "The Lord knoweth how to deliver the godly out of temptations, and to reserve the unjust unto the day of judgment to be punished:"

I Thessalonians 5:9 "For God hath not appointed us to wrath, but to obtain salvation by our Lord Jesus Christ,"

Revelation 3:10 "Because thou hast kept the word of my patience, I also will keep thee from the hour of temptation, which shall come upon all the world, to try them that dwell upon the earth.

I Corinthians 15:52 "In a moment, in the twinkling of an eye, at the last trump: for the trumpet shall sound, and the dead shall be raised incorruptible, and we shall be changed."

I Thessalonians 4:16-18
4:16 "For the Lord himself shall descend from heaven with a shout, with the voice of the archangel, and with the trump of God: and the dead in Christ shall rise first:"
4:17 "Then we which are alive *and* remain shall be caught up together with them in the clouds, to meet the Lord in the air: and so shall we ever be with the Lord."
4:18 "Wherefore comfort one another with these words."

The Church

Judgment begins with the church and not the world.

I Peter 4:17-18

4:17 "For the time *is come* that judgment must begin at the house of God: and if *it* first *begin* at us, what shall the end *be* of them that obey not the gospel of God?" 4:18 "And if the righteous scarcely be saved, where shall the ungodly and the sinner appear?"

It could be said a lost generation is preceded by a compromised church that has left its first love. A church lacking passion and conviction that has been tainted by the world. A church that has allowed false doctrine to come in and has gotten away from preaching holiness and the righteousness of God. A church that no longer feeds its people the word but starves them with sermonettes and motivational speeches. If this is a lost generation not taught the ways of the Lord, then who is to blame? Do we blame the children who looked to us for direction? The people who sought the church for deliverance. Is it not those who were entrusted with the gospel and charged with setting good examples and winning them to Christ? Just consider the divorce rate in the church is no different than the world and the many single Christian mothers who are raising young boys and girls in the absence of Christian fathers.

Consider state- of -the- art churches, that appear larger than life, with abundant wealth and resources, but the communities surrounding them are overrun with poverty and blight. Consider the watered-down messages, designed to attract members instead of building disciples, causing many people to leave out of the church the same way they walked in. The many celebrities we invite into the church to attract crowds followed by the hypocrisy of then telling our children not to buy their records or imitate their lifestyles. The many gifts and talents exploited while blindly ignoring the fruit of the individual making merchandise of the people for selfish gain. Consider the hypocrisy of preaching against rock stars and the excessiveness of the world, but then living like one with extravagant lifestyles and seeking worldly success and fame. The many Christians who use social media to post scriptures in the morning but then half-dressed pictures and ungodly behavior at night. We are all to blame, myself included. Not just for what we have done but what we have failed to do. The many times God could have used us to speak into someone's life, but we were too

235

preoccupied chasing after worldly things. The quality time we could have spent with our children, the relationships we could have restored, the sacrifices we could have made, the times we should have spoken up, and the godly examples we could have set. We see a day where professing Christians will pick up a sign because they hate the President but have never picked up a sign advocating for God. Again, these things are common to each of us, and we have all missed the mark, but judgment is a time of decision in which God is allowing us a sliver of time to get it right with Him. We must choose whether to defend and justify our behavior or to seek His face, humble ourselves and repent. Those who refuse to repent shall remain in their sins and be judged with this rebellious world, thus, experiencing the wrath of God. During times of judgment, it is the church that is put on the examination table.

Luke 5:31-32
5:31 "And Jesus answering said unto them, They that are whole need not a physician; but they that are sick."
5:32 "I came not to call the righteous, but sinners to repentance.

Judgment comes before wrath because it is God's merciful attempt to address the issues in the church, so it doesn't suffer the same fate as the world. In other words, the wrath of God is preceded by choice. God is longsuffering, and He loves us so much He warns us of the wrath to come and gives us space to repent. Just as in the days of Noah, we still have time to get into the ark. The moment we are in now, and it is the message that should be preached across every pulpit "repent for the time of the Lord is at hand." Seen in the Book of Revelation in the messages delivered to the seven churches. Here God is inspecting His church and acknowledges the things they are doing right while admonishing them for the things they need to address and clean up. The overall theme is He is warning them to repent so they will not be judged with the world. He is exposing the sin in the church for purification for only the righteous shall be spared. He is speaking to us, and we must take heed to His voice. The Lord is revealing what is really in our hearts so we can seek His face for deliverance and receive strength to turn away from those things which are not pleasing in His sight.

237

Often, we are not even aware of what is in our hearts, so the Lord brings things to our attention as He is doing in His message to the seven churches. Purification is a process of becoming more like Him. It involves not only dealing with sin but doubt and unbelief as well. It is developing blind trust in the Lord and having the faith to stand on His Word in every circumstance.

Jeremiah 17:9 "The heart *is* deceitful above all *things*, and desperately wicked: who can know it?"

I Corinthians 11:31-32
11:31 "For if we would judge ourselves, we should not be judged."
11:32 "But when we are judged, we are chastened of the Lord, that we should not be condemned with the world."

Revelation 18:4 "And I heard another voice from heaven, saying, Come out of her, my people, that ye be not partakers of her sins, and that ye receive not of her plagues."

Luke 8:12 "For nothing is secret, that shall not be made manifest; neither *any thing* hid, that shall not be known and come abroad.

Judgment reveals the faith of the church and the fear of the world

Faith is essential in times of Judgment because it is the only way to overcome fear. As world events unfold, people will experience more hopelessness, anxiety, depression, drug and alcohol addiction, and suicide. The root cause of this mental and emotional distress is fear and the uncertainty of the days we are in. It will be a time like none other in history when darkness shall descend upon the world. The Bible warns us times will be so bad men's hearts shall fail them as a result of fear and uncertainty.

Luke 21:26 "Men's hearts failing them for fear, and for looking after those things which are coming on the earth: for the powers of heaven shall be shaken."

Revelation 12:12 "Therefore rejoice, *ye* heavens, and ye that dwell in them. Woe to the inhabiters of the earth and of the sea! for the devil is come down unto you, having great wrath, because he knoweth that he hath but a short time"

Matthew 24:21 "For then shall be great tribulation, such as was not since the beginning of the world to this time, no, nor ever shall be."

Fear will pave the way for the anti-christ as people will be desperate for calm, security, and peace. The conditions will be ripe, and the anti-christ will appear to have an answer for the pain they feel, the peace they

yearn for, and the emptiness they are experiencing. This

generation is seeking a solution, not a savior so they

will accept and receive him. They will even receive his

mark and worship him as god.

Revelation 13:6-8
6:6 "And he opened his mouth in blasphemy against
God, to blaspheme his name, and his tabernacle, and
them that dwell in heaven."
6:7 "And it was given unto him to make war with the
saints, and to overcome them: and power was given him
over all kindreds, and tongues, and nations."
6:8 "And all that dwell upon the earth shall worship
him, whose names are not written in the book of life of
the Lamb slain from the foundation of the world."

As the judgment of God unfolds, the world will be

overcome with fear while the church delivered through

its faith. Faith is a supernatural process which connects

us to God by activating the power of the Living Word

inside of us. It is how the Lord delivers His people out

of temptations and preserves them from the

consequences of His wrath. Throughout the Bible, God

uses faith to deliver His people from impossible

situations and circumstances. Faith allows God to work

through us to accomplish the extraordinary. God is a

straight line, with no change at any point in the existence of the universe. He is constant and does not change with time. He is the same yesterday, today, and forever and His Word is sure. Only those who truly belong to God have Faith, and without faith, it is impossible to walk in fellowship with God. For faith, it is essential to have a relationship with Jesus Christ.

Hebrews 11:6 "But without faith *it is* impossible to please *him*: for he that cometh to God must believe that he is, and *that* he is a rewarder of them that diligently seek him."

When walking in faith, circumstances will often appear to get worse before they get better. We don't always know the full plan of God only the part He has revealed to us. We must trust God even when we can't see the big picture. At times He uses challenging circumstances to build and develop our faith and trust in Him and other times because He has a purpose in mind. Just consider the children of Israel when the Lord delivered them out of Egypt. As they approached the edge of the Red Sea Pharaohs army pursued hard behind them. The people were desperately afraid and feared for their lives. The impending danger exposed their unbelief as they began to doubt and panic. Each moment the army got closer, the people became more and more afraid as they looked at the reality of the situation as opposed to the awesome power of God.

Exodus 14:10-14
14:10 "And when Pharaoh drew nigh, the children of Israel lifted up their eyes, and, behold, the Egyptians marched after them; and they were sore afraid: and the children of Israel cried out unto the LORD."
14:11 "And they said unto Moses, Because *there were* no graves in Egypt, hast thou taken us away to die in the wilderness? wherefore hast thou dealt thus with us, to carry us forth out of Egypt?"
14:12 "*Is* not this the word that we did tell thee in Egypt, saying, Let us alone, that we may serve the Egyptians? For *it had been* better for us to serve the Egyptians, than that we should die in the wilderness."
14:13 "And Moses said unto the people, Fear ye not, stand still, and see the salvation of the LORD, which he will shew to you today: for the Egyptians whom ye have seen today, ye shall see them again no more forever."
14:14 "The LORD shall fight for you, and ye shall hold your peace."

What the children of Israel did not know was at the same time God was delivering them He was also judging Egypt. God was punishing Pharaoh for his sins and for the way he treated His people. The children of

Israel needed only to have faith in their deliverance. Although it was the same God that performed many miracles on their behalf and forced Pharaoh to let them go, the minute they faced adversity the doubt in their heart was revealed. It was God who allowed Pharaoh to closely pursue His people in order to destroy his entire army. As the children of Israel passed on dry land across the Red Sea, the waters came crashing down on Pharaoh's army. It didn't matter how great an empire Egypt was or how mighty its army; it was no match for the Almighty God who created the Heavens and the earth. In destroying Pharaoh's army, the people saw the mighty hand of God and reverenced His name.

Exodus 14:17-18

14:17 "And I, behold, I will harden the hearts of the Egyptians, and they shall follow them: and I will get me honour upon Pharaoh, and upon all his host, upon his chariots, and upon his horsemen."
14:18 "And the Egyptians shall know that I *am* the LORD, when I have gotten me honour upon Pharaoh, upon his chariots, and upon his horsemen."

Exodus 14:27-31

14:27 "And Moses stretched forth his hand over the sea, and the sea returned to his strength when the morning appeared; and the Egyptians fled against it; and the LORD overthrew the Egyptians in the midst of the sea."

243

14:28 "And the waters returned, and covered the chariots, and the horsemen, *and* all the host of Pharaoh that came into the sea after them; there remained not so much as one of them."

14:29 "But the children of Israel walked upon dry *land* in the midst of the sea; and the waters *were* a wall unto them on their right hand, and on their left."

14:30 "Thus the LORD saved Israel that day out of the hand of the Egyptians; and Israel saw the Egyptians dead upon the sea shore."

14:31 "And Israel saw that great work which the LORD did upon the Egyptians: and the people feared the LORD, and believed the LORD, and his servant Moses."

During times of judgment, we must always remember God has a blueprint, and Bible prophecy is the precise plan of God. Faith declares God is with us in our darkest hour. Even today, as Christian persecution is on the rise, more and more people are falling away from God, and it appears as if Satan is winning in a significant way the stage is being set for God to show Himself strong in the face of those who oppose Him. In other words, God is allowing the world to boast great things against Him, persecute His people, and enjoy a false sense of security for a season. During these perilous times, the church must focus on His promises despite what we hear and see as the world continues to become more defiant. It is going to make laws restricting religious freedom, it is going to act in rebellion, and it is going to oppose the Bible and attack the people who believe in it. We are in a time of judgment where God will sit back and allow it to happen no different than when Pharaoh pursued the children of Israel, but He has a purpose in mind. Just know at the appointed time the waters will again come crashing down. Stay focused on God and trust He is in absolute control. He has a plan and timeline only He knows. He is merciful, and all men left without excuse. At the Day of Judgment, He will rewind the tape in the presence of His enemies who will bow before His throne reminded of their proud words, ungodly acts, and debauchery. He will remind them of every opportunity they were given to repent and turn from their wicked ways. He will remind them how He watched His people suffer at their expense that they would come to know He is a merciful God. Then He will appoint them their place in the Lake of Fire where they shall spend eternity suffering for their sins. So, in essence, they have been given a few seconds to make a decision that will last through eternity.

I Peter 1:7 "That the trial of your faith, being much more precious than of gold that perisheth, though it be tried with fire, might be found unto praise and honour and glory at the appearing of Jesus Christ:"

II Peter 3:8-10

3:8 "But, beloved, be not ignorant of this one thing, that one day *is* with the Lord as a thousand years, and a thousand years as one day."

3:9 "The Lord is not slack concerning his promise, as some men count slackness; but is longsuffering to us-ward, not willing that any should perish, but that all should come to repentance.

3:10 "But the day of the Lord will come as a thief in the night; in the which the heavens shall pass away with a great noise, and the elements shall melt with fervent heat, the earth also and the works that are therein shall be burned up."

Judgment is a time of separation

Another purpose of judgment is to separate the Body of Christ from the children of the world. Particularly within the Body itself. The Bible speaks about the sheep and the goats and the wheat and the tares. God's people are referred to as the sheep and the wheat. Many people confess the name of Christ, but their hearts not surrendered to Him. They use His name, attend churches, and claim to know Him, but these are merely outward expressions and gestures made in vain. The Bible warns us unless you know Him in your heart, you are none of His. Judgment reveals the true love we have in our heart and is demonstrated by keeping His commandments and living boldly in His name. Those who truly love Him will not deny Him in the face of adversity, and He will stand for them and confess their names before the Father. They will suffer and reign with Him. Those who belong to Him are connected through His Spirit and not deceived by the wickedness in this world. They will be people of faith that trust solely in His voice, which is the Bible, the unadulterated Word of God.

John 10:27 "My sheep hear my voice, and I know them, and they follow me:"

John 10:4-5
10:4 "And when he putteth forth his own sheep, he goeth before them, and the sheep follow him: for they know his voice."
10:5 "And a stranger will they not follow, but will flee from him: for they know not the voice of strangers."

Matthew 13:30 "Let both grow together until the harvest: and in the time of harvest I will say to the reapers, Gather ye together first the tares, and bind them in bundles to burn them: but gather the wheat into my barn."

II Corinthians 6:17-18
6:17 "Wherefore come out from among them, and be ye separate, saith the Lord, and touch not the unclean *thing*; and I will receive you,"
6:18 "And will be a Father unto you, and ye shall be my sons and daughters, saith the Lord Almighty."

Matthew 10:32 "Whosoever therefore shall confess me before men, him will I confess also before my Father which is in heaven."

Luke 9:23 "And he said to *them* all, If any *man* will come after me, let him deny himself, and take up his cross daily, and follow me."

The danger of a watered-down word-deficient church is many people are sitting in the pews on the wrong side of Judgment. They are not being taught to deal with their sin and are in rebellion against God. Disillusioned into thinking they can live on both sides of the fence and their gifts and talents are a substitute for obedience and repentance. They sit back silent while other Christians are persecuted for their faith.

They preach lovely messages and are admired by the world while other pastors are labeled hateful for preaching the truth. Remaining silent and failing to take a stand is a form of denial, and those who deny Him will not have their names confessed before the Father. During times of judgment, there is no middle ground, and you either suffer with Him or continue enjoying the pleasures of the world seeking affirmation from men.

Matthew 7:21-23
7:21 "Not every one that saith unto me, Lord, Lord, shall enter into the kingdom of heaven; but he that doeth the will of my Father which is in heaven."
7:22 "Many will say to me in that day, Lord, Lord, have we not prophesied in thy name? and in thy name have cast out devils? and in thy name done many wonderful works?"
7:23 "And then will I profess unto them, I never knew you: depart from me, ye that work iniquity."

Mark 7:6-7
7:6 "He answered and said unto them, Well hath Esaias prophesied of you hypocrites, as it is written, This people honoureth me with *their* lips, but their heart is far from me."
7:7 "Howbeit in vain do they worship me, teaching *for* doctrines the commandments of men."

Luke 9:26 "For whosoever shall be ashamed of me and of my words, of him shall the Son of man be ashamed, when he shall come in his own glory, and *in his* Father's, and of the holy angels."

Matthew 10:33 "But whosoever shall deny me before men, him will I also deny before my Father which is in heaven."

Galatians 1:10 "For do I now persuade men, or God? or do I seek to please men? for if I yet pleased men, I should not be the servant of Christ."

I stated earlier America is more divided now than ever before, but not all divisions are the product of men. The violent and vile behavior we have witnessed at some of the protests across the country is not just a reflection of their anger towards a person or group but a mirror of what exists in their hearts. In other words, the days will reveal what is truly in a man's heart, meaning a hateful person responds with hate because hate is in him, a lewd person responds with lewdness, a disorderly person responds with disorder, and a violent person responds with violence. Regardless of the offense, whatever is in your heart will determine how you react. The Bible says a person is known by their fruits or the behavior they exhibit, and there is nothing hidden that shall not be made known. During a time of judgment, our hearts will be exposed, at times by Satan other times by God, and we must all give an account for the words we speak and the way we live. People are not your excuse for acting ungodly and whatever is in your heart is being exposed. The days ahead will show you who you are. The Bible tells us we must all work out our salvation with fear and trembling meaning no one owes you anything in this life and at all times we are personally responsible to God for how we act, what we say, and how we think. There are no victims in Heaven because all have sinned and come short of His glory.

Luke 8:17 "For nothing is secret, that shall not be made manifest; neither *any thing* hid, that shall not be known and come abroad."

Revelation 22:11 "He that is unjust, let him be unjust still: and he which is filthy, let him be filthy still: and he that is righteous, let him be righteous still: and he that is holy, let him be holy still.

Matthew 24:10 "And then shall many be offended, and shall betray one another, and shall hate one another.

Matthew 12-34-37
12:34 "O generation of vipers, how can ye, being evil, speak good things? for out of the abundance of the heart the mouth speaketh."

12:35 "A good man out of the good treasure of the heart bringeth forth good things: and an evil man out of the evil treasure bringeth forth evil things."

12:36 "But I say unto you, That every idle word that men shall speak, they shall give account thereof in the day of judgment."

12:37 "For by thy words thou shalt be justified, and by thy words thou shalt be condemned."

Philippians 2:12 "Wherefore, my beloved, as ye have always obeyed, not as in my presence only, but now much more in my absence, work out your own salvation with fear and trembling."

The closer we get to the return of Jesus Christ, the sharper the division will be between those who fear God and obey His commandments and those who do not. You can already see it in some of the political discourse and marches. The messages on the signs increasingly point to a common enemy subtilty disguised in their rhetoric. The day fast approaches when you will see the common enemy is God. It will transcend race, politics, economic status, and culture as God begins to draw His Spirit out of this world. The more the world is given over to the gods they have chosen to serve the less polite and unrestrained the conversations will be. It will spark fear in the hearts of those who merely honor Him with their lips but a revival in the hearts of those who truly love Him pushing them to become more intimately and personally connected to Him. Throughout the Bible, adversity has served as a wakeup call causing God's people to be more sensitive to His voice.

Matthew 10:34-39

10:34 "Think not that I am come to send peace on earth: I came not to send peace, but a sword."

10:35 "For I am come to set a man at variance against his father, and the daughter against her mother, and the daughter in law against her mother in law."

10:36 "And a man's foes *shall be* they of his own household."

10:37 "He that loveth father or mother more than me is not worthy of me: and he that loveth son or daughter more than me is not worthy of me."

10:38 "And he that taketh not his cross, and followeth after me, is not worthy of me."

10:39 "He that findeth his life shall lose it: and he that loseth his life for my sake shall find it."

Judgment begins with you and your house

We live in a day of great deception, and many will fall away trusting their logic and reasoning as opposed to strict reliance on the Word of God. The Body of Christ is a collection of families representing God in the earth. Regardless of the various assignments

253

and duties we have, our first ministry is our home. To endure the days we are in, we must be intentional and deliberate how we walk in the face of our children, how we love and treat our spouses and the representation of Christ we show the world. It must be reflected on the job, demonstrated on social media, and it must govern the decisions we make, the people we support, and who and what we, stand for. We must be conscious of spiritual warfare and give no place to the enemy to influence our hearts and minds. In other words, who you stand for and with matters and regardless of the sentiment in the world, you cannot choose sides with them. You must stand for God irrespective of your political affiliations, race, culture, or economic status. You are responsible for the company you keep, the messages you support, the words you allow on your page, the people you march with, and the words that come out of your mouth. The enemy will look for compromises and inconsistencies in your life to pull you away from the word, which results in commonality with the world. Remember you don't have to know the plan, you simply have to live by it. The world is building a tower, and they need you to supply the bricks. Every compromise is a brick. Jesus said Satan had nothing in Him, meaning there was nothing He could accuse Him of nor was there any sin he could attach to Him. Veering from the Word gives Satan legal authority and access in your life.

John 14:30 "Hereafter I will not talk much with you: for the prince of this world cometh, and hath nothing in me."

Again, we cannot operate as the world does regardless as to our personal feelings and emotions. One example of this is how Christians respond to politics. This issue has not only divided the nation; it has even divided the church. Christians may not agree on politics, but we should all agree on the Word of God. For example, we see Christians who are unwilling to pray for the president and express the same disrespect and disdain for him as those who are in the world. Regardless as to our personal views and opinions, the Bible is the final authority which unites us, but more and more Christians are finding common ground with those who share their personal beliefs as opposed to biblical beliefs. The Bible has become a guide instead of a principal, a book of suggestions as opposed to instructions for life. The less reverence and fear we have for the Word of God, the more susceptible we will be to deception. You will find yourself marching right next to people who are at the same time mocking Jesus and demeaning the Bible in the name of a common enemy or cause. Despite what you see, think, and feel, you do not know the mind of God, nor do you understand all of His plans.

Isaiah 55:8
55:8 "For my thoughts *are* not your thoughts, neither *are* your ways my ways, saith the LORD."
55:9 "For *as* the heavens are higher than the earth, so are my ways higher than your ways, and my thoughts than your thoughts."

Consider King Nebuchadnezzar, who ruled the pagan Babylonian Empire. By all accounts, this was a very evil and wicked man. He conquered the nation of Israel, the apple of God's eye, destroyed and desecrated the temple, spoiled their land, and took the people captive who had not been killed. He is the same king who had the three Hebrew Boys thrown into a burning fiery furnace after they refused to worship an idol, he built unto himself. Based on his resume, this is the last man God would use, but the Bible tells us it was God that delivered Judah into his hand. Judgment came upon Judah for its idolatry and doing evil in the sight of God after being warned but failing to repent.

Daniel 1:1-2
1:1 "In the third year of the reign of Jehoiakim king of Judah came Nebuchadnezzar king of Babylon unto Jerusalem, and besieged it."
1:2 "And the Lord gave Jehoiakim king of Judah into his hand, with part of the vessels of the house of God: which he carried into the land of Shinar to the house of his god; and he brought the vessels into the treasure house of his god."

We follow the Word of God regardless of our thoughts and feelings because we only see the beginning of a matter where God sees the end. Just as God had a plan for Pharaoh, He also had a plan for Nebuchadnezzar, but this time it wasn't to destroy him. Instead, He humbled the king, and his heart was turned towards Him.

Daniel 4:34-37
4:34 "And at the end of the days I Nebuchadnezzar lifted up mine eyes unto heaven, and mine understanding returned unto me, and I blessed the most High, and I praised and honoured him that liveth for ever, whose dominion *is* an everlasting dominion, and his kingdom *is* from generation to generation:"

4:35 "And all the inhabitants of the earth *are* reputed as nothing: and he doeth according to his will in the army of heaven, and *among* the inhabitants of the earth: and none can stay his hand, or say unto him, What doest thou?"

4:36 "At the same time my reason returned unto me; and for the glory of my kingdom, mine honour and brightness returned unto me; and my counsellors and my lords sought unto me; and I was established in my kingdom, and excellent majesty was added unto me.

4:37 "Now I Nebuchadnezzar praise and extol and honour the King of heaven, all whose works *are* truth, and his ways judgment: and those that walk in pride he is able to abase.

Here we see King Nebuchadnezzar giving God more praise at the end of his life than some Christians have. This once wicked King, who made an idol of himself and desecrated the Temple of God, now blessed the Most High and gave Him honor and praise, acknowledging Him as the King of Heaven. The point is God can do all things and uses whoever He chooses to fulfill His will. Because we do not know the mind of God, we must trust Him and do as His Word instructs us. Jesus died so all men can repent and be saved. It does not mean you have to support everything the president does or agree with the way he lives his life.

You should respect the office and sincerely pray for him the same way someone prayed for you before you gave your life to Christ. It amazes me how people can believe for a house with bad credit and no money in the bank, but no faith to believe God can change a man's heart. Do not be deceived by what you see simply stand on the Word of God.

I Timothy 2:1-4
2:1 "I exhort therefore, that, first of all, supplications, prayers, intercessions, *and* giving of thanks, be made for all men;"
2:2 "For kings, and *for* all that are in authority; that we may lead a quiet and peaceable life in all godliness and honesty."
2:3 "For this *is* good and acceptable in the sight of God our Saviour;"
2:4 "Who will have all men to be saved, and to come unto the knowledge of the truth."

The Judgment of the World

Romans 1:18 "For the wrath of God is revealed from heaven against all ungodliness and unrighteousness of men, who hold the truth in unrighteousness;"

Once the church has been inspected, and men given space to repent comes the wrath of God or the judgment of the world in which it is punished for its rebellion and sin. God has a set time in which He leaves the door open to draw men to repentance. In other words, you don't just decide to come to God because a carnal heart cannot repent. Many people believe they can stop sinning and come to God when they get it all out of their system or become bored first. They liken it to be a switch that can be turned off and on, but it is God who draws us to Christ. The Bible tells us to heed to His voice because there is no guarantee you will ever hear it again. It is a precious thing when God is tugging at your heart, and at that moment, a decision must be made.

Hebrews 3:7-8
3:7 "Wherefore (as the Holy Ghost saith, Today if ye will hear his voice,"
3:8 "Harden not your hearts, as in the provocation, in the day of temptation in the wilderness:

John 6:43-44
6:43 "Jesus therefore answered and said unto them, Murmur not among yourselves."
6:44 "No man can come to me, except the Father which hath sent me draw him: and I will raise him up at the last day."

Matthew 4:17 "From that time Jesus began to preach, and to say, Repent: for the kingdom of heaven is at hand."

When we refuse to honor God, He withdraws His conviction and allows the consequences of sin to run its natural course. In other words, He no longer stands in the way of the darkness which opens the flood gates of sin into our lives. This condition is known as reprobation, which means you no longer have a conscious for God, nor can you appreciate the obvious signs of deterioration in your life or the consequences you must pay for your sin. The wrath of God is a consequence of man's choice.

Romans 1:24-32
1:24 "Wherefore God also gave them up to uncleanness through the lusts of their own hearts, to dishonour their own bodies between themselves:"
1:25 "Who changed the truth of God into a lie, and worshipped and served the creature more than the Creator, who is blessed for ever. Amen."
1:26 "For this cause God gave them up unto vile affections: for even their women did change the natural use into that which is against nature:"
1:27 "And likewise also the men, leaving the natural use of the woman, burned in their lust one toward another; men with men working that which is

261

unseemly, and receiving in themselves that recompence of their error which was meet."
1:28 "And even as they did not like to retain God in *their* knowledge, God gave them over to a reprobate mind, to do those things which are not convenient;"
1:29 "Being filled with all unrighteousness, fornication, wickedness, covetousness, maliciousness; full of envy, murder, debate, deceit, malignity; whisperers,"
1:30 "Backbiters, haters of God, despiteful, proud, boasters, inventors of evil things, disobedient to parents,"
1:31 "Without understanding, covenantbreakers, without natural affection, implacable, unmerciful:"
1:32 "Who knowing the judgment of God, that they which commit such things are worthy of death, not only do the same, but have pleasure in them that do them."

Sin hardens the heart and the Bible states that even in the light of God's wrath, evil men will still not repent of their rebellion and wickedness.

Revelation 9:20-21
9:20 "And the rest of the men which were not killed by these plagues yet repented not of the works of their hands, that they should not worship devils, and idols of gold, and silver, and brass, and stone, and of wood: which neither can see, nor hear, nor walk:"
9:21 "Neither repented they of their murders, nor of their sorceries, nor of their fornication, nor of their thefts."

262

Again, the wrath of God is not intended for the church, but those who do not repent and take heed to His ways. Those who contend a loving God would not impose such consequences upon His people have no understanding of why God must eradicate sin. The first reason is God is light and has no darkness in Him. Even when His Only Begotten Son, Jesus Christ, hung on the cross for our sins, God turned His back on Him. For those moments, our sins were laid upon Him, and He was separated from the Father for the first time because there is no sin in God. The second reason is sin is the plague, a toxic destroyer wiping out everything in its path. Even the earth itself deteriorates under the weight of sin. If God did not judge sin, it would devour everything it touches.

Matthew 27:46 "And about the ninth hour Jesus cried with a loud voice, saying, Eli, Eli, lama sabachthani? that is to say, My God, my God, why hast thou forsaken me?"

Romans 8:22-23
8:22 "For we know that the whole creation groaneth and travaileth in pain together until now. "
8:23 " And not only *they*, but ourselves also, which have the firstfruits of the Spirit, even we ourselves

263

groan within ourselves, waiting for the adoption, *to wit*, the redemption of our body.

The wrath of God comes when sin has reached its pinnacle. Consider the flood during Noah's day. The Bible tells us the entire earth was filled with violence, and the thoughts and imaginations of man's heart were evil continually. Despite Noah warning the people for several years and building the monumental ark, only Noah and his family had not been consumed by sin. Not one person outside of his family repented of their sin, and the Bible says all flesh had been corrupted.

Genesis 6:5-6
6:5 "And GOD saw that the wickedness of man *was* great in the earth and *that* every imagination of the thoughts of his heart *was* only evil continually."
6:6 "And it repented the LORD that he had made man on the earth, and it grieved him at his heart.

Genesis 6:11-13
6:11 "The earth also was corrupt before God, and the earth was filled with violence."
6:12 "And God looked upon the earth, and, behold, it was corrupt; for all flesh had corrupted his way upon the earth."
6:13 "And God said unto Noah, The end of all flesh is come before me; for the earth is filled with violence through them; and, behold, I will destroy them with the earth.

Genesis 7:5-7

7:5 "And Noah did according unto all that the LORD commanded him."

7:6 "And Noah *was* six hundred years old when the flood of waters was upon the earth."

7:7 "And Noah went in, and his sons, and his wife, and his sons' wives with him, into the ark, because of the waters of the flood."

Consider the cities of Sodom and Gomorrah where sin had gotten so bad the Bible says every man in the city, both young and old, surrounded the house of Lot determined to rape the angels that came to visit him. The men were unaware they were angels and sought to know or have sex with the men. Sin had gotten so bad every single male young and old gathered at the house to participate in this rape. Again, only Lot and his family saved from God's wrath.

Genesis 19:4-5

19:4 "But before they lay down, the men of the city, *even* the men of Sodom, compassed the house round, both old and young, all the people from every quarter:"

19:5 "And they called unto Lot, and said unto him, Where *are* the men which came in to thee this night? bring them out unto us, that we may know them.

Genesis 19:24-25

19:24 "Then the LORD rained upon Sodom and upon Gomorrah brimstone and fire from the LORD out of heaven;"

19:25 "And he overthrew those cities, and all the plain, and all the inhabitants of the cities, and that which grew upon the ground."

This is the real face of the days we are living in today where we have begun to open the flood gates for sin and immorality. We have set on a course of rebellion, and there is no end in sight. Where there is no Word, there is no restraint, nor is there any fear of God. As old voices die off and we diminish the role and respect, we once held for parents and seniors the ways of God are all but forgotten, and there is no one to remind us of His ways. As new politicians emerge who view the Bible as an impediment to progress, restriction on freedom, and a divisive tool, both intolerant and hateful, the further we descend. They are unaware and misinformed concerning the true nature of our nation's success, despising even the country that afforded them so much opportunity. They are naïve to the plots and schemes of our enemies who watch as we implode and do very little to protect ourselves based on partisanship

266

and hidden agendas. They are ignorant of history and why great empires like Rome fell and have little regard for protecting the most vulnerable among us. They do not know the role of the family and the impact of its decline. We are a nation divided and a society that is steep in sin, from the young to the old. Sin permeates our culture, has corrupted our institutions, destroyed our families, and now not even the children are safe. They are being hypersexualized and bombarded with ungodly influences.

Isaiah 5:13-14

5:13 "Therefore my people are gone into captivity, because *they have* no knowledge: and their honourable men *are* famished, and their multitude dried up with thirst."

5:14 "Therefore hell hath enlarged herself, and opened her mouth without measure: and their glory, and their multitude, and their pomp, and he that rejoiceth, shall descend into it."

The time for this nation's judgment has come, and the Lord will avenge the blood of the millions of babies sacrificed. You see there is nothing new under the sun and the only difference between the sacrifices then and the sacrifices now is they are done in clinics as opposed to on an altar or in a temple for all to see. But even still the Lord's compassion is extended to His people despite the graveness of the offense but instead of repenting and turning from our wicked ways we have become bolder and more arrogant even passing new laws which push the envelope even further in defiance of the Most High God.

Judgment is God repaying the wicked for the crimes they have committed against His children

God knows every hair on the heads of His children. Above all things, He is a compassionate and loving Father who loves us more than we could ever imagine. He set us above the Angels, gave His only Begotten Son to die on our behalf, and has forgiven us for the most egregious betrayals and sin. The Bible says it is better to be drowned by a gigantic boulder in the depths of the sea than to harm those that love and trust in Him. God will have the last word where His children are concerned. Despite the persecution, rape, murder, imprisonment, and torture of millions of Christians around the world God is in absolute control, and He remembers every tear, witnesses every offense, counts the days of their affliction, and sets His eyes upon the pain His children experience in this world. These impossible circumstances can only be endured through the assistance of the Holy Ghost and miraculous power of God. Throughout history, millions of Christians have paid the ultimate price for their faith. The question asked why a loving God would allow such things? The Bible leads me to believe there are at least two reasons for such hardship and affliction. The first is the agape love God has for man and His desire that all men would choose to be in a relationship with Him. He is long-suffering in the face of the atrocities committed by wicked men giving them space to repent and turn back to Him.

The spilled blood of His children is not taken lightly and cries out to him from the ground demanding vengeance. The Bible states, "Vengeance is mine, I will repay," says God, meaning there are no cold cases in Heaven and every drop of innocent blood accounted for at the Day of Judgment. Including, the blood of unborn babies taken from the womb. The Bible says that life is in the Blood, not the size or trimester of the fetus, so from the moment there is a trace of Blood, there is life.

269

This Blood shall stand as a witness against those who have shed it. Again, even in the case of innocent Blood, the vengeance of God is balanced by the righteous Blood of His Son Jesus Christ that cries out for mercy in the face of judgment. Those who receive it and turn from their sins shall obtain forgiveness.

The second reason God does not avenge His children readily is He does not view death the same way we do. Death is a transition in which the mortal becomes immortal and the corruptible incorruptible. The way we die does not alter how we transition from this life. From the moment we are born into this fallen world, unless we are raptured, death is a certainty. The apostle Paul said, "to die is gain." God is faithful to His children until the very end, and even in death, He is with us waiting to welcome us home. On the other side of death is eternal life and just as the martyr, Stephen did, as he was being stoned, and the countless others who paid the ultimate price, we must have faith and trust in Him. The Bible says death is a defeated foe and has no power or grip over God's people so what we think we see is not really what we see, and faith is the supernatural bridge between reality and the supernatural power of God. In other words, it's no different than any other miracle; what people experience in the natural has nothing to do with what is happening in the spirit realm. As he was dying, *Stephen* prayed to God to receive his spirit and further asked God not to hold the sin against his killers. *Stephen* then "fell asleep" or died. What man could utter such things in his own strength?

Considering this, God has an appointed time in which He will avenge the Blood of His children. The wrath of God will be swift upon those who have harmed and persecuted them.

Luke 12:7 "But even the very hairs of your head are all numbered. Fear not therefore: ye are of more value than many sparrows."

Matthew 18:6-7
18:6 "But whoso shall offend one of these little ones which believe in me, it were better for him that a millstone were hanged about his neck, and *that* he were drowned in the depth of the sea."
18:7 "Woe unto the world because of offences! for it must needs be that offences come; but woe to that man by whom the offence cometh!"

Luke 18:7-8
18:7 "And shall not God avenge his own elect, which cry day and night unto him, though he bear long with them?"
18:8 "I tell you that he will avenge them speedily. Nevertheless when the Son of man cometh, shall he find faith on the earth?"

Genesis 4:-9-10
4:9 "And the LORD said unto Cain, Where *is* Abel thy brother? And he said, I know not: *Am* I my brother's keeper?"
4:10 "And he said, What hast thou done? the voice of thy brother's blood crieth unto me from the ground."

Philippians 1:20-21
1:20 "According to my earnest expectation and *my* hope, that in nothing I shall be ashamed, but *that* with all boldness, as always, *so* now also Christ shall be magnified in my body, whether *it be* by life, or by death."
1:21 "For to me to live *is* Christ, and to die *is* gain."

Revelation 6:9-11
6:9 "And when he had opened the fifth seal, I saw under the altar the souls of them that were slain for the word of God, and for the testimony which they held:"
6:10 "And they cried with a loud voice, saying, How long, O Lord, holy and true, dost thou not judge and avenge our blood on them that dwell on the earth?"
6:11 "And white robes were given unto every one of them; and it was said unto them, that they should rest yet for a little season, until their fellowservants also and

their brethren, that should be killed as they *were*, should be fulfilled."

Revelation 19:1-3
19:1 "And after these things I heard a great voice of much people in heaven, saying, Alleluia; Salvation, and glory, and honour, and power, unto the Lord our God:"
19:2 "For true and righteous *are* his judgments: for he hath judged the great whore, which did corrupt the earth with her fornication, and hath avenged the blood of his servants at her hand"
19:3 "And again they said, Alleluia. And her smoke rose up for ever and ever."

Acts 7:54-60
7:54 "When they heard these things, they were cut to the heart, and they gnashed on him with *their* teeth."
7:55 "But he, being full of the Holy Ghost, looked up stedfastly into heaven, and saw the glory of God, and Jesus standing on the right hand of God"
7:56 "And said, Behold, I see the heavens opened, and the Son of man standing on the right hand of God."
7:57 "Then they cried out with a loud voice, and stopped their ears, and ran upon him with one accord,"
7:58 "And cast *him* out of the city, and stoned *him*: and the witnesses laid down their clothes at a young man's feet, whose name was Saul."
7:59 "And they stoned Stephen, calling upon *God*, and saying, Lord Jesus, receive my spirit."
7:60 "And he kneeled down, and cried with a loud voice, Lord, lay not this sin to their charge. And when he had said this, he fell asleep."

Leviticus 17:11 "For the life of the flesh *is* in the blood: and I have given it to you upon the altar to make an atonement for your souls: for it *is* the blood *that* maketh an atonement for the soul."

John 15:20-21
15:20 "Remember the word that I said unto you, The servant is not greater than his lord. If they have persecuted me, they will also persecute you; if they have kept my saying, they will keep yours also."
15:21 "But all these things will they do unto you for my name's sake, because they know not him that sent me."

Things will get increasingly worse in this world

During the last days, things will get increasingly worse because evil and wickedness will be unrestrained the moment God removes His light out of the earth. The only thing standing in the way of total anarchy and depravity is the light of the church that is still present in the earth. It is what holds back the onslaught of evil waiting to overtake the world. The church is filled with the Spirit of God and is His restraining power in the earth but as it drifts further away from the Word of God the dam is starting to crack, and the darkness is becoming increasingly dark. The more watered down and compromising the church grows, the less power it possesses to restrain the darkness. Despite some of its brightness being dulled, God still works through His faithful remnant who continue to stand in opposition to the powers of darkness. While this remnant remains in the earth, the power of its prayers and faith in God's word hinders the works of the enemy and frustrates his plans. Again, this is why he works day and night to destroy God consciousness to dim the light that exists in the world. For every saint who gives over to the flesh, another flame has been extinguished.

The day fast approaches the trumpet will sound, and the withholding power of the church moved out of the way, and then the full brunt of Satan's power will be felt, and his diabolical agenda revealed. Not only will God remove His people, but He shall send strong delusion into the minds of those who perish that they will believe the lie the antichrist presents to the world. The Tribulation period, marked by a brief period of peace and then sudden destruction and calamity like never witnessed upon the earth. There shall be death, plagues, famine, devastation in the land and the sea, terror in the skies above, and violent earthquakes and lawlessness. In addition to these catastrophic events, the tyranny and cruelty of the anti-christ and false religious leader shall be imposed upon them during their brutal and wicked reign.

II Thessalonians 2:5-10
2:5 "Remember ye not, that, when I was yet with you, I told you these things?"
2:6 "And now ye know what withholdeth that he might be revealed in his time."
2:7 "For the mystery of iniquity doth already work: only he who now letteth *will let*, until he be taken out of the way."
2:8 "And then shall that Wicked be revealed, whom the Lord shall consume with the spirit of his mouth, and shall destroy with the brightness of his coming:"
2:9 "*Even him*, whose coming is after the working of Satan with all power and signs and lying wonders,"
2:10 "And with all deceivableness of unrighteousness in them that perish; because they received not the love of the truth, that they might be saved."
2:11 "And for this cause God shall send them strong delusion, that they should believe a lie:"
2:12 "That they all might be damned who believed not the truth, but had pleasure in unrighteousness."

Revelation 12:12 "Therefore rejoice, *ye* heavens, and ye that dwell in them. Woe to the inhabiters of the earth and of the sea! for the devil is come down unto you, having great wrath, because he knoweth that he hath but a short time."

I Thessalonians 5:3 "For when they shall say, Peace and safety; then sudden destruction cometh upon them, as travail upon a woman with child; and they shall not escape."

After the great tribulation, is the Battle of Armageddon, in which the Lord, called Faithful and True, shall descend from Heaven, returning with His armies to put an end to those who are destroying the earth. The Second Coming of Christ in which He returns to the earth with His church to establish His kingdom. The Rapture and The Second Coming are two separate events occurring independently of another. At the time of the Lord's return, the church has already been raptured and returns with Him to destroy the armies of the wicked. Satan's forces are utterly destroyed, and the anti-christ and false prophet are cast alive into the Lake of Fire.

Revelation 19:11-16;19-21

19:11 "And I saw heaven opened, and behold a white horse; and he that sat upon him *was* called Faithful and True, and in righteousness he doth judge and make war."

19:12 "His eyes *were* as a flame of fire, and on his head *were* many crowns; and he had a name written, that no man knew, but he himself."

19:13 "And he *was* clothed with a vesture dipped in blood: and his name is called The Word of God."

19:14 "And the armies *which were* in heaven followed him upon white horses, clothed in fine linen, white and clean."

19:15 "And out of his mouth goeth a sharp sword, that with it he should smite the nations: and he shall rule them with a rod of iron: and he treadeth the winepress of the fierceness and wrath of Almighty God."

19:16 "And he hath on *his* vesture and on his thigh a name written, KING OF KINGS, AND LORD OF LORDS."

19:19 "And I saw the beast, and the kings of the earth, and their armies, gathered together to make war against him that sat on the horse, and against his army."

19:20 "And the beast was taken, and with him the false prophet that wrought miracles before him, with which he deceived them that had received the mark of the beast, and them that worshipped his image. These both were cast alive into a lake of fire burning with brimstone."

19:21 "And the remnant were slain with the sword of him that sat upon the horse, which *sword* proceeded out of his mouth: and all the fowls were filled with their flesh."

After the tribulation period, Satan is bound for one thousand years in the bottomless pit. He is not allowed to deceive the nations until the thousand years of peace and tranquility is fulfilled. Then there will be a time of joy and laughter where people shall live in peace and harmony with one another. The Lord shall reign over them with His saints and men will learn war no more. This period is known as the Millennial Reign. After these thousand years, Satan is loosed for a short period before staging his last but feeble rebellion against the Most High God. Satan's armies devoured, and he is cast into the Lake of Fire with the anti-christ and False Prophet to be tormented day and night forever.

Revelation 20:1-3
20:1 "This will be followed by the thousand-year millennial reign which is a time of peace for all nations. 20:2 "And he laid hold on the dragon, that old serpent, which is the Devil, and Satan, and bound him a thousand years,"
20:3 "And cast him into the bottomless pit, and shut him up, and set a seal upon him, that he should deceive the nations no more, till the thousand years should be fulfilled: and after that, he must be loosed a little season."

Revelation 20:7-10
20:7 "And when the thousand years are expired, Satan shall be loosed out of his prison,"
20:8 "And shall go out to deceive the nations which are in the four quarters of the earth, Gog and Magog, to gather them together to battle: the number of whom *is* as the sand of the sea."

279

20:9 "And they went up on the breadth of the earth, and compassed the camp of the saints about, and the beloved city: and fire came down from God out of heaven, and devoured them."
20:10 "And the devil that deceived them was cast into the lake of fire and brimstone, where the beast and the false prophet *are*, and shall be tormented day and night for ever and ever."

All these events lead up to the most significant time in history. The time in which all of God's creation shall stand before His throne and give an account for the lives they have lived. This event is known as The Great White Throne Judgment, which determines where each of us will spend eternity. It is the formal sentencing where the rolls officially read from the Lamb's Book of life sealing the fate of the wicked and declaring God's mercy upon all those whose names contained therein. Because all men have sinned and fallen short of the glory of God, we are all guilty before His throne, meaning none of us can withstand God's judgment, and we would all suffer the same fate. The difference lies in the Blood of Jesus Christ and God's offer of mercy for all that would repent and receive it. Those who are covered by the Blood are not judged.

Like the death angel that was sent through the land of
Egypt, claiming the lives of every first-born child who
was not in a home covered by the Blood, death, and
judgment shall claim the lives of all who are not
covered by the Blood of Jesus at the Day of Judgment.
When death descended upon the land, it passed over
every house that was covered by the Blood. The same
will occur at the Great White Throne; every soul that is
covered by Jesus Blood shall be passed over. Those
who are not covered by the Blood shall be judged and
found guilty as charged. They will be cast into the Lake
of Fire where they shall spend eternity. This is the
second death or spiritual death, which is eternal
separation from God. Hell and all of its inhabitants are
cast into the Lake of Fire and those written in the
Lambs Book of Life are granted eternal life with the
Father. Hell is like the county jail; it is a temporary
holding facility where men await their trial. The Lake
of Fire is like a prison where men are sent once they
have their day in court and judged and sentenced. In
this case, there is only one sentence, which is life
without the possibility of parole. It is dreadful, it is

indescribable, it is the most horrific and terrifying event imaginable, and it is final. Imagine being brought out of the torments of Hell briefly, where the fire is not quenched and the worm dieth not, only to be formally judged and sent to a worse place for all eternity is beyond belief.

If you are reading these words, you still have a choice where you will spend eternity. Do you want to roll the dice putting your faith in the voices of dying men who oppose God while trusting in mere money, status, and fame? Or the sound of the handlers enticing the mob down a path with no end in sight? Or will you trust in the God of Heaven whose word stands in the face of countless generations of men boasting great things and then returning to the dust of the earth? The same Word that describes with precision the world in which you now live whose validity continues to defy mathematical probabilities and equations. This word has given you a warning concerning the days which lie ahead and now is your time of decision.

Philippians 2:10-11

2:10 "That at the name of Jesus every knee should bow, of *things* in heaven, and *things* in earth, and *things* under the earth;"
2:11 "And *that* every tongue should confess that Jesus Christ *is* Lord, to the glory of God the Father."

Revelation 20:14-15

20:11 "And I saw a great white throne, and him that sat on it, from whose face the earth and the heaven fled away; and there `was found no place for them."
20:12 "And I saw the dead, small and great, stand before God; and the books were opened: and another book was opened, which is *the book* of life: and the dead were judged out of those things which were written in the books, according to their works."
20:13 "And the sea gave up the dead which were in it; and death and hell delivered up the dead which were in them: and they were judged every man according to their works."
20:14 "And death and hell were cast into the lake of fire. This is the second death."
20:15 "And whosoever was not found written in the book of life was cast into the lake of fire."

A Real Place Called Hell

Whether you read the Old or New Testament, whether you consider the writings of the prophets, the teachings of Jesus Christ, or the epistles of the apostles, you will find there is only one conclusion concerning a place called Hell. **It is real**. Many of the things discussed in this chapter will build on the foundation already established concerning the fall of Lucifer, and the fall of man. In a day where sound doctrine is under attack, and more and more people are looking for loopholes to live on both sides of the fence, this discussion is a matter of Eternal security in the Body of Christ. Increasingly, people are being led astray by a distorted perception of God's love, which excuses man's fallen nature as opposed to dealing with it. The belief Hell doesn't exist is often fueled by the proposition a loving God would not impose such dire consequences on His creation. Some preachers refuse to preach about Hell or even sin for that matter.

Hell is not a message of fear, as some would have you believe, but a message of God's grace and mercy. Other than the gift of God giving His only Begotten Son, Jesus Christ, I do not feel there is any more magnificent illustration of mercy and grace than God making a way of escape for fallen man. God doesn't send people to Hell; instead, He saves people from going by offering them a choice to be redeemed. He desires no man to go to Hell. People choose to go there by refusing to surrender to Him. The message people need to hear is "Hell is a conscious choice" and not an inevitable conclusion.

Hell is a place of eternal punishment and separation from the presence of God, and regardless of how bad things get in life, it is not a condition which exists on earth. It has a physical location. Throughout the Bible, scores of scriptures illustrate the realities of Hell and here are a few facts to consider:

I. The Bible tells us Hell is a place of torment and suffering.

Luke 16:19-24
16:19 "There was a certain rich man, which was clothed in purple and fine linen, and fared sumptuously every day:"

16:20 "And there was a certain beggar named Lazarus, which was laid at his gate, full of sores,"
16:21 "And desiring to be fed with the crumbs which fell from the rich man's table: moreover the dogs came and licked his sores."
16:22 "And it came to pass, that the beggar died, and was carried by the angels into Abraham's bosom: the rich man also died, and was buried;"
16:23 "And in hell he lift up his eyes, being in torments, and seeth Abraham afar off, and Lazarus in his bosom."
16:24 "And he cried and said, Father Abraham, have mercy on me, and send Lazarus, that he may dip the tip of his finger in water, and cool my tongue; for I am tormented in this flame."

Matthew 25:41; 46
25:41 "Then shall he say also unto them on the left hand, Depart from me, ye cursed, into everlasting fire, prepared for the devil and his angels:"
25:46 "And these shall go away into everlasting punishment: but the righteous into life eternal."

II. Hell was created for Satan and the angels who followed him in his rebellion against God.

The following scriptures also give us insight concerning God's attitude towards iniquity. We know God loved Lucifer from the spectacular beauty and deliberation that went into his creation; however, the iniquity within him, resulted in eternal separation from

286

God. As stated earlier, a common theme of those who deny Hell is real is, "A loving God would not send a person to Hell." I agree wholeheartedly. God's love does not send a person to Hell, but iniquity will result in a person going straight to Hell.

Isaiah 14:12-15
14:12 "How art thou fallen from heaven, O Lucifer, son of the morning! [how] art thou cut down to the ground, which didst weaken the nations!"
14:13 "For thou hast said in thine heart, I will ascend into heaven, I will exalt my throne above the stars of God: I will sit also upon the mount of the congregation, in the sides of the north:"
14:14 "I will ascend above the heights of the clouds; I will be like the most High."
14:15 "Yet thou shalt be brought down to hell, to the sides of the pit."

Ezekiel 28:14-18
28:14 "Thou [art] the anointed cherub that covereth; and I have set thee [so]: thou wast upon the holy mountain of God; thou hast walked up and down in the midst of the stones of fire."
28:15 "Thou [wast] perfect in thy ways from the day that thou wast created, till iniquity was found in thee."
28:16 "By the multitude of thy merchandise they have filled the midst of thee with violence, and thou hast sinned: therefore I will cast thee as profane out of the mountain of God: and I will destroy thee, O covering cherub, from the midst of the stones of fire."

287

28:17 "Thine heart was lifted up because of thy beauty, thou hast corrupted thy wisdom by reason of thy brightness: I will cast thee to the ground, I will lay thee before kings, that they may behold thee."
28:18 "Thou hast defiled thy sanctuaries by the multitude of thine iniquities, by the iniquity of thy traffick; therefore will I bring forth a fire from the midst of thee, it shall devour thee, and I will bring thee to ashes upon the earth in the sight of all them that behold thee."

III. Hell was enlarged due to the condition of man's unrepentant heart resulting from his fallen nature.

Isaiah 5:13-14
5:13 "Therefore my people are gone into captivity, because [they have] no knowledge: and their honourable men [are] famished, and their multitude dried up with thirst."
5:14 "Therefore hell hath enlarged herself, and opened her mouth without measure: and their glory, and their multitude, and their pomp, and he that rejoiceth, shall descend into it."

Proverbs 27:20 "Hell and destruction are never full; so the eyes of man are never satisfied."

When man fell in the garden, it was a conscious choice. His only hope to again dwell in the presence of a holy God was dying to his old nature and being born again in the new nature of Jesus Christ. This could only

288

occur by him exercising his free will and making a conscious choice to surrender to Him. You cannot merely know His name or accidentally take hold of salvation. It is a decision.

Man left to his own devices is deceitful and set on a course of wickedness. It is because of this nature; Hell was enlarged to contain the fallen men who choose to follow Satan in his rebellion against God. If there is no hell, then the implication is man's nature was redeemed by default, and the earth is nothing more than a snapshot of Heaven. If there is no prerequisite to surrender to Christ, then the moment He shed His Blood, the nature of man would have changed, and all men would have adopted His character. This idea is inconsistent with the words and teachings of Jesus Christ.

Matthew 10:34-38:
10:34 "Think not that I am come to send peace on earth: I came not to send peace, but a sword."
10:35 "For I am come to set a man at variance against his father, and the daughter against her mother, and the daughter in law against her mother in law."
10:36 "And a man's foes [shall be] they of his own household."

10:37 "He that loveth father or mother more than me is not worthy of me: and he that loveth son or daughter more than me is not worthy of me."
10:38 "And he that taketh not his cross, and followeth after me, is not worthy of me."

His purpose was not to bring peace to the earth, but a sword of division separating God's children from the devils. He came to deliver His people out of this wicked world and warned us of the extreme wickedness that would exist in the days before His coming. Men would be divided based on their acceptance or rejection of Him. In the book of Luke, He told His disciples conditions would be the same as in the days of Noah.

Luke 17:26-27
17:26 "And as it was in the days of Noe, so shall it be also in the days of the Son of man."
17:27 "They did eat, they drank, they married wives, they were given in marriage, until the day that Noe entered into the ark, and the flood came, and destroyed them all."

The conditions which existed in the days of Noah, described in the book of Genesis, was extremely wicked, and the earth filled with violence. All one has to do is turn on the news and see we are living in similar days. Unspeakable acts are being committed regularly.

(The Earth then)

Genesis 6:5-7; 11-12
6:5 "And GOD saw that the wickedness of man [was] great in the earth, and [that] every imagination of the thoughts of his heart [was] only evil continually."
6:6 "And it repented the LORD that he had made man on the earth, and it grieved him at his heart."
6:7 "And the LORD said, I will destroy man whom I have created from the face of the earth; both man, and beast, and the creeping thing, and the fowls of the air; for it repenteth me that I have made them."
6:11 "The earth also was corrupt before God, and the earth was filled with violence."
6:12 "And God looked upon the earth, and, behold, it was corrupt; for all flesh had corrupted his way upon the earth."

(The Earth now)

II Timothy 3:1-5; 13
3:1 "This know also, that in the last days perilous times shall come."
3:2 "For men shall be lovers of their own selves, covetous, boasters, proud, blasphemers, disobedient to parents, unthankful, unholy,"
3:3 "Without natural affection, trucebreakers, false accusers, incontinent, fierce, despisers of those that are good,"

3:4 "Traitors, heady, highminded, lovers of pleasures more than lovers of God;"
3:5 "Having a form of godliness, but denying the power thereof: from such turn away."
3:13 "But evil men and seducers shall wax worse and worse, deceiving, and being deceived."

IV. The final destination of the wicked is the Lake of Fire.

Hell and those that are in it shall be cast into the Lake of Fire for all eternity.

Revelation 20:14-15
20:14 "And death and hell were cast into the lake of fire. This is the second death."
20:15 "And whosoever was not found written in the book of life was cast into the lake of fire."

V. Jesus Christ is the way of escape.

The death, burial, and resurrection of our Lord and Savior Jesus Christ did not do away with Hell, grant man a license to live outside the will of God, take away his choice and free will, or render the judgment of God a moot point. What the work of the Cross did was open the door universally for all men to come back into fellowship with God, thus offering a way of escape from the consequences of Hell and death that had us bound.

Is it too unreasonable a request, in the light of all God did, all He gave up, and all He sacrificed, to require man turn from his wicked ways? Of course not. Instead, men refuse to surrender their lives to God because they enjoy unrighteousness.

John 3:18-19
3:18 "He that believeth on him is not condemned: but he that believeth not is condemned already, because he hath not believed in the name of the only begotten Son of God."
3:19 "And this is the condemnation, that light is come into the world, and men loved darkness rather than light, because their deeds were evil."

It should be obvious the debate concerning Hell is not fueled by a genuine misunderstanding over what the Bible says. It is rooted in excuses used to justify man's unwillingness to change his choices. For the redeemed man, Hell is no longer an issue.

John 3:16-17
3:16 "For God so loved the world, that he gave his only begotten Son, that whosoever believeth in him should not perish, but have everlasting life."

3:17 "For God sent not his Son into the world to condemn the world; but that the world through him might be saved."

I. Corinthians 15:22 "For as in Adam all die, even so in Christ shall all men be made alive."

The critical words in this verse are "in Christ," which lets us know you can also be "out of Christ." According to the Bible, the prerequisite for salvation is a person must be found "in Christ." It does not say through Jesus Christ all men go to Heaven. The Bible further describes what it means to be in Christ in the following scriptures:

II Corinthians 5:17 "Therefore if any man [be] in Christ, [he is] a new creature: old things are passed away; behold, all things are become new."

Romans 8:1 "[There is] therefore now no condemnation to them which are in Christ Jesus, who walk not after the flesh, but after the Spirit."

Consider the following passages taken from the books of Revelation and Ephesians. The Bible plainly states there are people "out of Christ" who will have no place in the Kingdom of God. It is also important to point out these words were spoken after Christ died for our sins, meaning His death was not blanket immunity from sin.

Revelation 21:8 "But the fearful, and unbelieving, and the abominable, and murderers, and whoremongers, and sorcerers, and idolaters, and all liars, shall have their part in the lake which burneth with fire and brimstone: which is the second death."

Revelation 20:15 "And whosoever was not found written in the book of life was cast into the lake of fire."

Ephesians 5:5-6
5:5 "For this ye know, that no whoremonger, nor unclean person, nor covetous man, who is an idolater, hath any inheritance in the kingdom of Christ and of God."
5:6 "Let no man deceive you with vain words: for because of these things cometh the wrath of God upon the children of disobedience."
5:7 "Be not ye therefore partakers with them."

The term "in Christ" is synonymous with "the Kingdom of God," and the term "out of Christ" with the "Kingdom of Satan." In I. Corinthians 15:24, we see the ultimate purpose of Jesus Christ dying on the Cross was to deliver the Kingdom back to God.

I. Corinthians 15:24 "_Then [cometh] the end, when he shall have delivered up the kingdom to God, even the Father; when he shall have put down all rule and all authority and power."

There are scores of references, illustrations, and parables used to describe God's Kingdom, and the distinction between His Kingdom and Satan's Kingdom. There are two very different Kingdoms operating in the earth, one eternally connected to God or "in Christ," and one eternally separated from Him or "out of Christ." Both Kingdoms are comprised of the souls of men who have exercised their choice and free will. Jesus, Himself, made this distinction when addressing a group of people who thought they were righteous but had no part in Him.

John 8:39-44

8:39 "They answered and said unto him, Abraham is our father. Jesus saith unto them, If ye were Abraham's children, ye would do the works of Abraham."

8:40 "But now ye seek to kill me, a man that hath told you the truth, which I have heard of God: this did not Abraham."

8:41 "Ye do the deeds of your father. Then said they to him, We be not born of fornication; we have one Father, [even] God."

8:42 "Jesus said unto them, If God were your Father, ye would love me: for I proceeded forth and came from God; neither came I of myself, but he sent me."

8:43 "Why do ye not understand my speech? [even] because ye cannot hear my word."

8:44 "Ye are of [your] father the devil, and the lusts of your father ye will do. He was a murderer from the beginning, and abode not in the truth, because there is no truth in him. When he speaketh a lie, he speaketh of his own: for he is a liar, and the father of it."

It is important to note in the above passage Jesus knew who He was talking with. There are those that may argue these men had not yet been redeemed because the work of the Cross had not yet been completed; however; Jesus knew all things. He knew the hearts of every man and whether they would receive Him or not. The Bible says in John 10:14, "I am the good shepherd, and know my [sheep], and am known of mine." Jesus knew who His sheep were even before He went to the Cross.

Luke 13: 24-28
13:24 "Strive to enter in at the strait gate: for many, I say unto you, will seek to enter in, and shall not be able."
13:25 "When once the master of the house is risen up, and hath shut to the door, and ye begin to stand without, and to knock at the door, saying, Lord, Lord, open unto us; and he shall answer and say unto you, I know you not whence ye are:"
13:26 "Then shall ye begin to say, We have eaten and drunk in thy presence, and thou hast taught in our streets."

13:27 "But he shall say, I tell you, I know you not whence ye are; depart from me, all [ye] workers of iniquity."
13:28 "There shall be weeping and gnashing of teeth, when ye shall see Abraham, and Isaac, and Jacob, and all the prophets, in the kingdom of God, and you [yourselves] thrust out."

In Matthew 13, Jesus spoke to His disciples concerning the final separation, which would occur at the Day of Judgment after the work of the Cross was completed. He called His children wheat and the children of the devil tares.

Matthew 13:37-43
13:37 "He answered and said unto them, He that soweth the good seed is the Son of man;"
13:38 "The field is the world; the good seed are the children of the kingdom; but the tares are the children of the wicked [one];"
13:39 "The enemy that sowed them is the devil; the harvest is the end of the world; and the reapers are the angels."
13:40 "As therefore the tares are gathered and burned in the fire; so shall it be in the end of this world."
13:41 "The Son of man shall send forth his angels, and they shall gather out of his kingdom all things that offend, and them which do iniquity;"
13:42 "And shall cast them into a furnace of fire: there shall be wailing and gnashing of teeth."

13:43 "Then shall the righteous shine forth as the sun in the kingdom of their Father. Who hath ears to hear, let him hear."

Now consider the doctrine of inclusion which refutes the existence of hell. Some proponents suggest the following passages in I. Corinthians 15:27-28 speak to the ultimate subjection of man's will to God, resulting in universal salvation for all men. They go on to say since all men will confess Christ at the Day of Judgment, they must be saved because men can only confess Christ by the Holy Spirit. Such a conclusion confuses the concepts of surrender and subjection. The critical distinction is subjection describes the dominion of God at the Day of Judgment, where surrender describes the dominion of man to exercise choice and free will on earth. Salvation requires surrender and can only occur as a result of man choosing God as opposed to being subjected to Him.

I. Corinthians 15:27-28
15:27 "For he hath put all things under his feet. But when he saith all things are put under [him, it is] manifest that he is excepted, which did put all things under him."

15:28 "And when all things shall be subdued unto him, then shall the Son also himself be subject unto him that put all things under him, that God may be all in all."

From the beginning, man was given the right to exercise choice and free will. Whether to accept or reject God has always been his decision. The day is approaching when man will stand before Him in judgment and give an account for his choices. Satan and the angels who followed his rebellion will also answer to God. At this moment, God will exercise His absolute authority over all His creation by bringing everything into total subjection to Him.

Revelation 20:11-13
20:11 "And I saw a great white throne, and him that sat on it, from whose face the earth and the heaven fled away; and there was found no place for them."
20:12 "And I saw the dead, small and great, stand before God; and the books were opened: and another book was opened, which is [the book] of life: and the dead were judged out of those things which were written in the books, according to their works."
20:13 "And the sea gave up the dead which were in it; and death and hell delivered up the dead which were in them: and they were judged every man according to their works."

God will judge His creation by subduing and putting all things under His feet. It will no longer be a matter of choosing to surrender to God, but instead being subjected to His absolute authority. Salvation will have already been determined before man stands at the throne of God. In other words, it will be too late to choose God. Judgment is about being brought under subjection to the power and authority of the Almighty God, and not about giving you a choice.

Romans 14:11-12
14-11 "For it is written, [As] I live, saith the Lord, every knee shall bow to me, and every tongue shall confess to God."
14:12 "So then every one of us shall give account of himself to God."

Philippians 2:8-11
2:9 "Wherefore God also hath highly exalted him, and given him a name which is above every name:
2:10 "That at the name of Jesus every knee should bow, of [things] in heaven, and [things] in earth, and [things] under the earth;"
2:11 "And [that] every tongue should confess that Jesus Christ [is] Lord, to the glory of God the Father."

The time to choose salvation is now while the door is still open, and judgment delayed. Everyone who confesses Christ at the Day of Judgment will not be included in the Lamb's Book of Life, including Satan,

who will also acknowledge Jesus is Lord. His

confession will not be a result of choice, rather; a result

of being put under the subjection of the power of God.

Before Satan's kingdom is cast into the Lake of Fire, he

shall be stripped of all his authority, bow his knees to

the power of God, and confess the name of Jesus Christ.

Those who choose to follow Satan shall do the same as

the power of God binds and subjects them.

Mark 2:27 "No man can enter into a strong man's
house, and spoil his goods, except he will first bind the
strong man; and then he will spoil his house."

Revelation 20:10 "And the devil that deceived them
was cast into the lake of fire and brimstone, where the
beast and the false prophet [are], and shall be tormented
day and night for ever and ever."

Revelation 20:15 "And whosoever was not found
written in the book of life was cast into the lake of fire."

The more we investigate the Word of God, the

more apparent it becomes that those who deny the

existence of Hell are not using the Bible as their source.

As Christians, we must stick to the Bible and remember

the words of Jesus in Matthew 10:28, where He warned

men to fear the judgment of God. In other words, He warned us to put our trust, faith, and belief in the power of God as opposed to the deceit and limited wisdom of men.

Matthew 10:28 "And fear not them which kill the body, but are not able to kill the soul: but rather fear him which is able to destroy both soul and body in hell."

Jesus was straightforward when He spoke concerning sin and iniquity even denouncing some men by calling them the seed of the wicked, serpents, and vipers. He also spoke concerning the resurrection of the dead, the promises of God to the faithful and the judgment that would come to the wicked.

John 5:28-29
5:28 "Marvel not at this: for the hour is coming, in the which all that are in the graves shall hear his voice,"
5:29 "And shall come forth; they that have done good, unto the resurrection of life; and they that have done evil, unto the resurrection of damnation."

In II. Thessalonians, we see that after the work of the Cross was completed, the judgment of God still stood. This provides further proof the Blood of Jesus did not replace the judgment of God; instead, it created

303

an exception called mercy and grace for those who choose to receive it.

II. Thessalonians 1:7-9

1:7 "And to you who are troubled rest with us, when the Lord Jesus shall be revealed from heaven with his mighty angels,"

1:8 "In flaming fire taking vengeance on them that know not God, and that obey not the gospel of our Lord Jesus Christ:"

1:9 "Who shall be punished with everlasting destruction from the presence of the Lord, and from the glory of his power;"

1:10 "When he shall come to be glorified in his saints, and to be admired in all them that believe (because our testimony among you was believed) in that day."

So, what did Jesus Christ accomplish on the cross? Did He come to change the nature of God, or did He come to change the nature of men? Did His death excuse the fallen nature of man, or did it provide a solution for his fallen nature? Anyone who reads and believes in the Bible will conclude the death of Jesus Christ was God's plan to restore man to his original relationship before the fall. A covenant relationship between God and man based on choice, free will, and genuine love. A relationship governed by consequences and guided by God's instructions. A submissive relationship held together by obedience to His word, respect for His ways, and total trust in Him. A relationship motivated by the sincerity of the heart, a commitment to change, and a desire to be like Him. It is man coming to terms with his fallen nature and the realization his only hope is to be "in Christ." It is a choice to take responsibility for his actions, accept Jesus Christ as Lord and Savior, and surrender to His will.

In conclusion, Satan is a great deceiver, and his tactics have not changed since the Garden of Eden. The Bible states Jesus Christ is the way, the truth, and the life, and no man cometh to the Father but by Him. We must submit to God and His commandments and live by His will and not our own. Many people live as if the Blood of Jesus is a license to "do as thou wilt" because God's love doesn't judge, nor does it impose consequences. They take Hell entirely out of the Bible and claim those who advocate such a thing are full of hate. Be not deceived. The Bible says the consequences of refusing Him and His Word results in eternal separation.

Ultimately, we must either take God at His word or believe the lies of Satan. Do not be deceived by people who promise you carnal pleasure without consequences, and the opportunity to "do as thou wilt" while claiming you shall still see the face of God. Don't believe those who promote the false idea men are free to live outside of the design and order of God and still be assured of their place in Heaven. This thinking is distorted, self-serving, and in direct opposition to the will of God. It reduces Jesus Christ to a mere visionary who offered great words of encouragement and suggestions men could use to enjoy a higher quality of life while depicting Satan as nothing more than a spiritual hindrance with no real agenda other than to be a nuisance to man. Disobedience didn't work for Lucifer. It didn't work for Adam, and it won't work for you.

The message of Hell is a message of hope and good cheer for every man based on the understanding he must take responsibility for his actions. Where he goes when he takes his last breath is directly impacted by the choice he made while he was still living.

Ambassadors for Christ

II. Corinthians 5:14-16

5:14 "For the love of Christ constraineth us; because we thus judge, that if one died for all, then were all dead:"
5:15 "And [that] he died for all, that they which live should not henceforth live unto themselves, but unto him which died for them, and rose again."

It is our love for Christ, which compels our obedience and causes us to trust and believe in His word. The devil strives in the realm of logic and reason, so mere common sense isn't enough to defend against his deception. To have a genuine relationship with God, it takes faith and being led by His Spirit and Wisdom.

I Corinthians 1:18-21

1:18 "For the preaching of the cross is to them that perish foolishness; but unto us which are saved it is the power of God."
1:19 "For it is written, I will destroy the wisdom of the wise, and will bring to nothing the understanding of the prudent."
1:20 "Where [is] the wise? where [is] the scribe? where [is] the disputer of this world? hath not God made foolish the wisdom of this world?"

1:21 "For after that in the wisdom of God the world by wisdom knew not God, it pleased God by the foolishness of preaching to save them that believe."

Each chapter previously discussed in this book leads to the following conclusion: "God's solution to man's rebellion is the love He expressed in giving His only Begotten Son Jesus Christ." Our relationship with God and hope in eternal life is activated once we receive this love, which makes us whole in every area of our lives. It is because of this love we sacrifice our wants and desires to do His will.

I. **An Ambassador for Christ is a new creature.**

II. Corinthians 5:20-21
5:20 "Now then we are ambassadors for Christ, as though God did beseech [you] by us: we pray [you] in Christ's stead, be ye reconciled to God."
5:21 "For he hath made him [to be] sin for us, who knew no sin; that we might be made the righteousness of God in him."

To be an ambassador of Christ means we must let go of our old ways of thinking and embrace the mind of Christ. It is a process of sanctification or being cleansed and renewed through the knowledge of God. Consider the following verses:

308

Romans 12:2 "And be not conformed to this world: but be ye transformed by the renewing of your mind, that ye may prove what [is] that good, and acceptable, and perfect, will of God."

Ephesians 2:2
2:2 "Wherein in time past ye walked according to the course of this world, according to the prince of the power of the air, the spirit that now worketh in the children of disobedience:"

It means we no longer engage in a life of disobedience, which is the norm and custom of the world under the control and influence of Satan. Instead, we are restored to our right standing with God before the fall and live according to His plan, purpose, and design. The process is even more evident in the following passages of scripture:"

II. Corinthians 5:17 "Therefore if any man [be] in Christ, [he is] a new creature: old things are passed away; behold, all things are become new."

Ephesians 4:24 "And that ye put on the new man, which after God is created in righteousness and true holiness."

Colossians 3:10 "And have put on the new [man], which is renewed in knowledge after the image of him that created him:"

Ephesians 4:17-18

4:17 "This I say therefore, and testify in the Lord, that ye henceforth walk not as other Gentiles walk, in the vanity of their mind,"

4:18 "Having the understanding darkened, being alienated from the life of God through the ignorance that is in them, because of the blindness of their heart:"

When considering these verses together, we get a clear picture of what it means to be a new creature in Christ. If any man accepts the gift of Christ, he is made over in His righteousness and holiness. His mind is renewed and refreshed in the knowledge of God. His eyes open, and he receives the revelation of his true identity, which is the man he was created to be before the fall. He can see himself in the image of his Heavenly Father as having dominion and authority in the earth. He comes to the realization he has been blinded and deceived by Satan, puffed up in vanity, and has been alienated from the life God intended for him to have because of the iniquity he held in his heart.

Ephesians 4:22-23

4:22 "That ye put off concerning the former conversation the old man, which is corrupt according to the deceitful lusts;"

4:23 "And be renewed in the spirit of your mind;"

Upon receiving Christ, we are born again spiritually; however, the flesh must be crucified or put under subjection daily. Serving God is a choice, and each day, our commitment to Christ is renewed by surrendering our will to Him and abiding in His word. Once you give your life to Christ, the journey has only begun and merely saying you love Him will not guarantee your place in Heaven. You must be willing to serve Him with more than just your lips, and your actions must speak louder than your words. Saying "I do" does not make you a faithful spouse any more than fathering a child makes you a father if you refuse to be a part of the child's life. When we enter into covenant with Christ, our commitment is expressed through our obedience. Jesus said in John 14:15 "If ye love me, keep my commandments." Too many people are under the illusion the relationship ends at "I do" and are guilty of spiritual adultery. They do not understand to be married to God is to be divorced from the world.

Matthew 15:8 "This people draweth nigh unto me with their mouth, and honoureth me with [their] lips; but their heart is far from me."

Galatians 5:24 "And they that are Christ's have crucified the flesh with the affections and lusts."

James 4:4 "Ye adulterers and adulteresses, know ye not that the friendship of the world is enmity with God? whosoever therefore will be a friend of the world is the enemy of God."

Dying daily does not mean you will be perfect, and it is the Blood of Jesus, which keeps us connected to Him. Sanctification can be a challenging process at times, but when we fall short, we have an advocate in Heaven, the Lord Jesus Christ. We can call out on His name for mercy and forgiveness but must also be willing to repent and turn away from the sin to remain in fellowship with Him. Learning how to be like Christ also involves the humility to receive God's chastening, which is the correction He provides for those He loves.

I John 1:9 "If we confess our sins, he is faithful and just to forgive us [our] sins, and to cleanse us from all unrighteousness."

Hebrews 12:5-7
12:5 "And ye have forgotten the exhortation which speaketh unto you as unto children, My son, despise not thou the chastening of the Lord, nor faint when thou art rebuked of him:"

12:6 "For whom the Lord loveth he chasteneth, and scourgeth every son whom he receiveth."
12:7 "If ye endure chastening, God dealeth with you as with sons; for what son is he whom the father chasteneth not?"

Dying daily requires sacrifice, suffering, and constraints on personal gratification. Sacrifice means we must be willing to let go, suffering means we must endure through the trials of life, and constraint means voluntary restrictions on liberty. In the face of temptation and worldly influences, we choose the love of God and to walk in obedience to His word. Our commitment doesn't just end at refraining from sin but avoiding those things which can lead to sin as well.

I Corinthians 6:12 "All things are lawful unto me, but all things are not expedient: all things are lawful for me, but I will not be brought under the power of any."

We must learn to put limitations on our liberty. Often, it is the gray areas which cause us to stumble and lead us into sin. I'm speaking of those pesky little things which may not appear to be sinful in and of themselves, but are not in our best interest. Being an ambassador for Christ means we can't watch everything we see on T.V., go to every movie, or hang out with every person.

313

Some conversations we need to walk away from, some events we can't attend, some environments we need to avoid, some songs should never be sung, and some books should never be read.

Luke 21:34 "And take heed to yourselves, lest at any time your hearts be overcharged with surfeiting, and drunkenness, and cares of this life, and [so] that day come upon you unawares."

Sin can be subtle or overt, and the primary way we allow it in is through the choices we make with our eyes and ears. We can't expect to have victory over sin if we flood our mind and heart with worldly things. As much as is possible, we must avoid all appearances of evil, and if it doesn't edify God, we must refrain from those activities and associations.

To represent Christ, we must learn to listen to that inner voice, the Holy Spirit, which leads and guides us into all righteousness and truth. It is His voice which makes us uncomfortable in sinful environments and engaging in activities which do not edify God by speaking to our conscious and reminding us who we are in Christ. It is a dangerous thing to ignore that still small voice on the inside that convicts us and pricks our heart. That voice or conviction is the only thing that separates us from having a conscience (that feeling of knowing something is wrong) and having no conscience where sin is concerned. The Bible warns us not to ignore God (the still voice) and risk no longer being convicted of our sin. Once we lose our conscience, we develop a reprobate mind having no boundaries or remorse. We do whatever feels good to satisfy our flesh, whether it is right or wrong.

Romans 1:28 "And even as they did not like to retain God in [their] knowledge, God gave them over to a reprobate mind, to do those things which are not convenient;"

Note the choice is not made by God, instead; He ceases to convict the individual that chooses not to retain Him in his knowledge ("when you choose not to hear God's instruction and live by His Word"). In other words, you fully embrace a "Do as thou wilt" mentality, aligning yourself with Satan's rebellion, and seeking only to satisfy your flesh.

I Thessalonians 5:22 "Abstain from all appearance of evil."

I Corinthians 6:20 "For ye are bought with a price: therefore glorify God in your body, and in your spirit, which are God's."

Romans 12:1 "I beseech you therefore, brethren, by the mercies of God, that ye present your bodies a living sacrifice, holy, acceptable unto God, [which is] your reasonable service."

Being an ambassador of Christ means we represent His interest and not our own. We are called to be His voice in the earth. We become walking billboards advertising His goodness, infomercials concerning His love, and documentaries regarding the power of the gospel to transform lives. We set aside our goals, ambitions, and desires to embrace His. In other words, we can't love this life more than we do Christ or place more significance on temporal things then we do on Him. We may be required to walk away from something we love, to let go of something that makes us feel secure or make drastic changes in our life when things finally appear to be falling in place. Being convinced whatever we give up for God is our gain because we know all things work together for our good because we love Him and are lined up with His purpose.

Matthew 16:24 "Then said Jesus unto his disciples, If any [man] will come after me, let him deny himself, and take up his cross, and follow me."

John 12:25 "He that loveth his life shall lose it; and he that hateth his life in this world shall keep it unto life eternal."

Romans 8:28 "And we know that all things work together for good to them that love God, to them who are the called according to *his* purpose."

II. The Enduring Attitude of an Ambassador.

The apostle Paul discounted all his earthly accomplishments in comparison to his purpose in Christ. He understood what he had gained in Christ far outweighed anything he had done or could ever accomplish for himself.

Philippians 3:7-8
3:7 "But what things were gain to me, those I counted loss for Christ."
3:8 "Yea doubtless, and I count all things [but] loss for the excellency of the knowledge of Christ Jesus my Lord: for whom I have suffered the loss of all things, and do count them [but] dung, that I may win Christ,"

An ambassador is not ashamed to stand in the face of opposition. He does not waiver, bite his tongue, and back down from the position on which he stands. He stands when it is comfortable or uncomfortable and when it is popular or unpopular. He is steadfast, unmovable, and always busy representing the will of his Lord. He is consistent, and his words do not change depending on the conversation or forum. He is willing to sacrifice everything; being fully convinced nothing he has done for Christ is in vain. His eyes are fixed on a better reward, which gives him the strength to finish the race.

II. Timothy 1:12 "For the which cause I also suffer these things: nevertheless I am not ashamed: for I know whom I have believed, and am persuaded that he is able to keep that which I have committed unto him against that day."

As professing Christians, the time has come for us to count up the cost. We must get back to the foundation of our faith, the Bible, and fully consider the price which we must be willing to pay. We must get past the lip service, wearing crosses because they're fashionable, and haphazardly saying His name. We must turn away from the watered down, weak, societal depictions of our faith which promotes love with no accountability, sin with no consequences, salvation with no repentance, heaven with no hell, commitment with no responsibility, and the idea you can be saved without a Savior. In other words, the world wants a more appealing Cross with no blood on it and which doesn't offend. It wants a universal religion built on peace and self-gratification that puts man and his desires at the center of things.

Our relationship with the Cross has been infiltrated, and it's time to put our hands back to the plow. Either Christ is our Savior, or he was nothing more than a good man. He is either the Son of God or a confused blasphemer. The Bible is either 100% correct or an unreliable source subject to man's interpretation. **Luke14:27** "And whosoever doth not bear his cross, and come after me, cannot be my disciple."

To reiterate, being an ambassador is about sharing Christ with the world and continuing the work He started. Based on His examples, it is clear the gospel is an invitation as opposed to an ultimatum. Just as

Jesus never wavered from His belief and purpose, neither must we. He never watered down the words of His Father for His listeners to feel comfortable, nor did He compromise who He was so others would not be offended. Like Him, we can love people without agreeing with the things they do. Even our Lord Jesus Christ would be labeled an insensitive hate monger if He dared to speak the truth today.

We stand on the Word of God and represent His interest in the earth, or we don't. We are called to advocate for the sanctity of life, the institution of marriage, the family, compassion for the poor, and moral society. Not because we are on the left or the right, not because we are Republican or Democrat, not because we are liberal or conservative, but because **we are Christians**. We advocate for the will of God and give hope to the world there is salvation through Him. This is what it means to be His ambassador.

Philippians 2:12 "Wherefore, my beloved, as ye have always obeyed, not as in my presence only, but now much more in my absence, work out your salvation with fear and trembling."

Curtain Call

Hebrews 2:3-4
2:3 "How shall we escape, if we neglect so great
salvation; which at the first began to be spoken by the
Lord, and was confirmed unto us by them that heard
him;"
2:4 "God also bearing *them* witness, both with signs
and wonders, and with divers miracles, and gifts of the
Holy Ghost, according to his own will?"

Psalm 53:1 "The fool hath said in his heart, *There is* no
God. Corrupt are they, and have done abominable
iniquity: *there is* none that doeth good."

    Often, a curtain call marks the end of a great

performance when the cast returns to the stage to be

recognized by the audience. It is a moment of relief

where the performer is rewarded for the long hours,

sacrifice, hard work, and dedication that went into each

rehearsal, line memorized, note sung, choreographed

move, and scene. A journey riddled with frustrations

and setbacks, but ultimately the joy and satisfaction that

comes from hearing the roar of the crowd who affirms

them with their praise. For many of us, those moments

will be far and few in between, but the Bible warns that we shall all be judged for the performance of a lifetime. A curtain call if you will, the final stage where we shall all stand before the host of heaven and give an account for the lives we have lived. Everything from the cradle to the grave, the highs and lows, victories and defeats, good times and bad times presented before His throne. For some, there shall be sounds of joy as they hear the words "Well done my good and faithful servant," being spoken by the Most High God, but for others the grim and dark reality despite the awards they received in this life, there were no preparations made for the life after that.

II Corinthians 5:10 "For we must all appear before the judgment seat of Christ; that every one may receive the things done in *his* body, according to that he hath done, whether *it be* good or bad."

Revelation 20:11-12
20:11 "And I saw a great white throne, and him that sat on it, from whose face the earth and the heaven fled away; and there was found no place for them."
20:12 "And I saw the dead, small and great, stand before God; and the books were opened: and another book was opened, which is *the book* of life: and the dead were judged out of those things which were written in the books, according to their works."

The Bible declares the fool says in heart, "There is no God." The fool does not prepare for this moment, nor does he regard or fear God. In his arrogance, he denies the works of His hands and pridefully scoffs at His word and commandments. He sees the sun come up every morning at the appointed time, the mysterious yet captivating glow of the moon, the changing of seasons bringing hope and new life, but remains silent and refuses to give God praise. Others find comfort in their fame and material success as they are idolized by the countless fans who follow their every move and blindly cling to their every breath. They boast of their exploits, accolades, and awards as they live lustful and rebellious lives, deceiving and influencing the masses away from God's ways. They have bank accounts overflowing with riches but are spiritually bankrupt and have not prepared for this final stage. They are bold to do sin and have no fear of consequences selling their souls as a prop for their fame. As the applauds keep coming, the curtains keep closing and the fans keep cheering it appears as if the party will never end, but the Bible warns us not to be fooled by the illusion of time.

James 4:14 "Whereas ye know not what *shall be* on the morrow. For what *is* your life? It is even a vapour, that appeareth for a little time, and then vanisheth away."

II Peter 3:8 "But, beloved, be not ignorant of this one thing, that one day *is* with the Lord as a thousand years, and a thousand years as one day.

In life, we have been given a different script, some more difficult than others, but what unites us is one day we will all face the certainty of "One last Curtain Call." One final breath and all our accomplishments, material possessions, fans, and wealth will be things of the past. The earth will replace us with the next batch of performers ready to live out their few seconds of fame, as we stand before Him, ready or not, prepared or not, to answer for the lives we have lived. The God who put breathe in our bodies and at the appointed time takes it away will have the final say where we shall spend eternity. What will you say to Him at that moment? No more scripts to read, writers to prepare your speech and handlers to do damage control. No more lawyers to bail you out, fans to boost your ego, and publicist to create the perfect spin. No more goods and possessions, just you and the God you mocked and despised. The God you never thought you would see or answer too. The God who loved you, but you never loved Him back. One last Curtain call, One Final Performance, and that is just the first few seconds of eternity.

Understand, there is absolutely nothing else God can do for you at that moment, and your fate determined. Judgment sealed, it will not be changed. If you searched every corner of Heaven, you would find there is no more He has to give because in this life He gave you His all and held nothing back. He gave you the very best He had, His Only Begotten Son Jesus Christ. His mercies were unlimited, and you were given countless opportunities to repent and turn from your evil ways. He endured your rebellion and rejection and continued to reach out to you, even sending people across your path. The finality of that moment will bear witness to all He has done, all He has sacrificed, and everything He suffered out of His everlasting love for you, but you rejected Him in the face of carnal things.

Hebrews 2:1-4

2:1 "Therefore we ought to give the more earnest heed to the things which we have heard, lest at any time we should let *them* slip."

2:2 "For if the word spoken by angels was stedfast, and every transgression and disobedience received a just recompence of reward;"

2:3 "How shall we escape, if we neglect so great salvation; which at the first began to be spoken by the Lord, and was confirmed unto us by them that heard *him*"

2:4 "God also bearing *them* witness, both with signs and wonders, and with divers miracles, and gifts of the Holy Ghost, according to his own will?"

The Battle Ready Conclusion

Psalm 7:11 "God judgeth the righteous, and God is angry *with the wicked* every day."

The Bible assures us the Lord Jesus Christ is soon to return, preceded by the rapture of the church. In the twinkling of an eye, the Body of Christ shall be caught up, or removed from the earth, kept from the hour of temptation, the tribulation period. Many will be left behind because they did not take heed to His warnings, nor did they repent of their sins. Included, many who professed to know Him, but their hearts were far from Him.

I Thessalonians 4:16-18
4:16 "For the Lord himself shall descend from heaven with a shout, with the voice of the archangel, and with the trump of God: and the dead in Christ shall rise first:"
4:17 "Then we which are alive [and] remain shall be caught up together with them in the clouds, to meet the Lord in the air: and so shall we ever be with the Lord."
4:18 "Wherefore comfort one another with these words."

The Prophetic Dream

I was driving down the street with my wife and mother on a warm, breezy, sunny day. Everything appeared perfect, including the beautiful blue, cloudless sky. The sun was so impressive that it seemed to fill the air with specks of light.

As I gazed upward, I saw a row of airplanes approaching looking like rubber pencils wobbling in the sky. As they got closer, they suddenly began falling with great speed. The pilots appeared to be making every attempt to pull up, but a powerful force seemed to be forcing them down. I was petrified as they began crashing to the ground one by one on the opposite side of the street. The force was so overwhelming they broke into a million pieces. There was smoke and fire everywhere, as well as cars and buildings crushed by the planes.

One of the planes came so close the wing clipped my truck and sent it tumbling over. Astonished no one was hurt, we scrambled out and began running in fear along with hundreds of other people who had flooded the streets. There was utter confusion. Traffic had been brought to a halt as people abandoned their cars and ran for cover. Some so stricken with fear, they dropped dead while others were crushed by falling debris. Dead bodies and body parts stacked one on top of another, and the streets drenched with blood. The farther we ran, the more the bodies littered the street.

Glancing again into the sky, I saw a dark, red mist consume the sun and everything appeared to be covered by blood. I could hear people screaming in torment and pain. There was pink neon lightning that began streaking out of the sky, followed by a loud cracking sound. We began to run again, and I was suddenly engulfed by a bright white, blinding light. The light was so piercing I lost track of everything else around me. I no longer saw my wife and mother running beside me. All I could do was look into the light, and it was as if I was the only person in the world. I immediately knew to start praising the Lord. As I praised Him, I began to fade away, and I understood I was being raptured. Warmth encompassed me and consumed me.

I suddenly awoke out of my sleep, and the Holy Spirit instructed me to start praying for my family, loved ones, and friends who had not given their lives to Jesus. I did as instructed and prayed they would repent and surrender their lives to Him. He told me His coming would be sudden and without notice, and those that had not surrendered their lives to Him would be lost.

If you are a Christian and this sounds like a science fiction movie, it's time to do some serious soul searching in terms of what you are being fed spiritually. The Lord spoke extensively about watchfulness and being ready for His return. He even told us what the signs would be leading up to that great day and how to be prepared. Our present era is marked by great deception, and the Bible warns us people perish for lack of knowledge. If people truly knew how close we are to His return, Christianity would look a lot different than it does today. People would be more concerned about being left behind than the cares of this life. There would be less hypocrisy and living on both sides of the fence, Heaven would be filled with prayers of repentance as opposed to petitions for more stuff, and we wouldn't put off until tomorrow the things God ask us to do today. It would be easier to forgive and forget, and we would all be more mindful of walking in love. Mere motivational preaches and feel-good religion is going to result in a lot of people being unprepared and ill-informed. It is your responsibility to find a church which preaches all of God's word and prepares you to be ready when He comes.

The only question which remains is, "will you be ready when the last trumpet sounds and the absolute truth of God's word is revealed to all left behind?" At that moment, I wonder what the scholars and wise men will say. Will they suggest the rapture was nothing more than two atoms colliding again causing millions to disappear without a trace, or will they once again look to evolution and theorize Christians got bored being human and mysteriously evolved back into monkeys, making their escape to the jungle? I am sure there will be those who will claim aliens abducted us as a gift to mankind. Regardless of what the headlines will read, or the justifications proposed, man's logic will once again prove foolish when up against the omnipotence of God.

We live in a day where the book of Revelation and the prophecies in the book of Daniel are unfolding before our eyes. Increasingly, we see the formation of a society where Christian values are ridiculed and despised. More and more people are falling away from God and questioning whether He even exist? Indeed, the battle lines are drawn, the conversations less polite, and people are becoming more blatant in their disdain for the Christian way of life. The day fast approaches where the middle ground will cease to exist, and a series of events will finally determine whether the Bible is the unadulterated Word of God.

As more and more people lose hope, and the church perceived as self-absorbed and out of touch, they will begin to look to the world for answers and solutions. They will turn away from their faith as economic uncertainties mount, challenges arise, and a real experience with God seems to be a million miles away. As the world becomes more fragile, uncaring, and unpredictable, the stage is set for a new way of life, which on the surface promises security and offers hope and peace. A New World Order, as it is openly phrased, will be characterized by compromise, acceptance of a humanistic world view, and forfeiture of rights and national sovereignty.

The emergence of this order will not have God at its center, but a man of great charisma and tremendous influence whose voice will be heard around the world. He will have the ability to usher in temporary peace, be a man of vigorous diplomacy and political influence, and offer answers to problems no one can seem to fix. He shall exercise complete control over the economy, financial institutions, and the movements of men causing all who buy or sell to receive his mark or the number of his name. The Bible calls this man the anti-christ because he comes in the form of a lamb but is a ravenous wolf. He will present himself as the Messiah, the savior of the world, and be joined by a false prophet, a religious leader who will cause countless people to worship him. Both shall perform miracles and possess supernatural abilities that will move the emotions of men in awe of their power. Entire nations shall put their faith in him and blindly follow him down a path of sure and swift destruction.

Revelation 13:11-18

13:11 "And I beheld another beast coming up out of the earth; and he had two horns like a lamb, and he spake as a dragon."

13:12 "And he exerciseth all the power of the first beast before him, and causeth the earth and them which dwell therein to worship the first beast, whose deadly wound was healed."

13:13 "And he doeth great wonders, so that he maketh fire come down from heaven on the earth in the sight of men,"

13:14 "And deceiveth them that dwell on the earth by *the means of* those miracles which he had power to do in the sight of the beast; saying to them that dwell on the earth, that they should make an image to the beast, which had the wound by a sword, and did live."

13:15 "And he had power to give life unto the image of the beast, that the image of the beast should both speak, and cause that as many as would not worship the image of the beast should be killed."

13:16 "And he causeth all, both small and great, rich and poor, free and bond, to receive a mark in their right hand, or in their foreheads:"

13:17 "And that no man might buy or sell, save he that had the mark, or the name of the beast, or the number of his name."

13:18 "Here is wisdom. Let him that hath understanding count the number of the beast: for it is the number of a man; and his number *is* Six hundred threescore *and* six."

Revelation 14:9-12

14:9 "And the third angel followed them, saying with a loud voice, If any man worship the beast and his image, and receive *his* mark in his forehead, or in his hand,"

14:10 "The same shall drink of the wine of the wrath of God, which is poured out without mixture into the cup of his indignation; and he shall be tormented with fire and brimstone in the presence of the holy angels, and in the presence of the Lamb:"

14:11 "And the smoke of their torment ascendeth up for ever and ever: and they have no rest day nor night, who worship the beast and his image, and whosoever receiveth the mark of his name."

14:12 "Here is the patience of the saints: here *are* they that keep the commandments of God, and the faith of Jesus."

Considering how grim the picture appears to be, we must remember God always has a remnant of dedicated people who remain faithful to the very end, never ceasing to proclaim His name. God will never be outdone, and even in a day, where so many people seem to be abandoning their faith, there are those whose faith has never been stronger. The tougher the times, the more their confidence grows for they are steadfast and anchored in Him. These are those who have overcome the world's image of Christianity, and the hypocrisy of religious exercises and going through the motions.

Be encouraged, for God has equipped us with everything we need to endure the days in which we live. We have access to God through our relationship with Jesus Christ and kept by the awesome power of the Holy Ghost. The three essential habits demonstrated in every believer's lifestyle are Praise and Thanksgiving, Holiness, and Prayer.

I. Praise and Thanksgiving

Psalm 100:1-4
100:1 "Make a joyful noise unto the LORD, all ye lands."
100:2 "Serve the LORD with gladness: come before his presence with singing."
100:3 "Know ye that the LORD he *is* God: *it is* he *that* hath made us, and not we ourselves; *we are* his people, and the sheep of his pasture."
100:4 "Enter into his gates with thanksgiving, *and* into his courts with praise: be thankful unto him, *and* bless his name."
100:5 "For the LORD *is* good; his mercy *is* everlasting; and his truth *endureth* to all generations."

I Thessalonians 5:18 "In every thing give thanks: for this is the will of God in Christ Jesus concerning you."

When we give God praise and thanksgiving, we recognize His absolute authority over Heaven and earth

336

and having all things under His feet. We acknowledge Him as Supreme in Authority and reminded of His attributes and ability to do all things. As we praise Him, we recognize He is greater than the challenges we face.

Praise gives us access to things which are unseen and allows us to enter the very courts of God. Through praise, we recognize and embrace the design, purpose, and will of God by acknowledging the works of His hands. It gives us peace during the storm, order in utter chaos, sanity in insanity, and a purpose in a world which has lost its way. In other words, we see a God who can deliver His people during times of famine, who gives light in darkness, and grants victory when the battle is all but lost. Praise removes the ceilings in our lives by taking off limitations and reminding us we don't have to be a product of our environment. Where we start doesn't determine where we end because we can do all things through Christ who strengthens us.

Thanksgiving builds our faith in God as we consider all the things He continues to do for us daily. Things we take for granted, call coincidences, consider

337

mere luck, and take credit for ourselves. His blessings are so abundant and plentiful; we become desensitized to all the miracles we witness every second of the day. Our minds are incapable of processing the many works He performs. Thanking God opens our eyes and enables us to see Him more and more. When you live a life of thanksgiving, it is easy to recognize He is not a million miles away because you began to see Him in everything you do. It is a relationship builder, and the more we thank Him, the more we experience the depths of His love.

It also helps us to understand His mercy because it gives us a glimpse into the many wonderful blessings we didn't deserve or even know how to ask. It helps us to feel special and affords us greater self-esteem by letting us know we have a Father who loves and cares for us every minute of the day, and that we are not accidents or mishaps. Every single life has a purpose and value in Him, and all these blessings are made possible through Thanksgiving.

We take so much for granted: the breath which gives us life, the beating of our heart, the miracle of

338

birth, the countless times He has held back death, accidents, unforeseen circumstances and events, dangers unseen, the complex systems which make our bodies work, a sound mind, and the ability to give and receive love. Without thanksgiving, people tend to develop amnesia, forgetting, and discounting Him and even denying His existence.

The Bible says the days before His return will be so disturbing and hopeless that men's hearts will fail them for fear and for looking after those things which are coming to pass.

Luke 21:26 "Men's hearts failing them for fear, and for looking after those things which are coming on the earth: for the powers of heaven shall be shaken.

In other words, the changes will be rapid and drastic, including economic collapse, catastrophic events, pestilences and disease, violent weather changes, earthquakes, social evils, wars and rumors of wars, violence, and depravity. The resulting stress, fear, anxiety, worry, and hopelessness will be overbearing, leading to heart attacks and robbing men of their will to live. Where there is no faith, there is fear, and the more our society takes its eyes off God, the scarier things will get.

In the days leading up to the rapture, our lives must be anchored in Him. Praise and Thanksgiving will give you the peace to walk on water during violent storms. It is the way we keep our eyes on Him as opposed to the raging of the waves and tossing of the waters in life.

II. Holiness

Holiness, our cloak of protection, in an ungodly and immoral world, allows God to operate in our lives and closes the door of satanic attack. It separates us from the children of the world and enables the light of Christ to shine brightly in us. Holiness is operating in the character of Christ by surrendering our will to His. It is a lifestyle which keeps us pure in God's eyes and untainted by the world. It does not mean we are perfect, in and of ourselves, or that we will no longer make mistakes in life. We are perfected in Christ and deemed pure in the eyes of God by the Blood of Jesus. To have a lifestyle of holiness, we must be in Christ and operating according to His word.

I Peter 1:13-16
1:13 "Wherefore gird up the loins of your mind, be sober, and hope to the end for the grace that is to be brought unto you at the revelation of Jesus Christ;"
1:14 "As obedient children, not fashioning yourselves according to the former lusts in your ignorance:"
1:15 "But as he which hath called you is holy, so be ye holy in all manner of conversation;"
1:16 "Because it is written, Be ye holy; for I am holy."

We live in a day where we must be watchful and ready for the Lord's return. Sin is a distraction and will result in our heart being unchecked and given over to the cares of this life, resulting in our being left behind when the Lord raptures the church. People are deceived when they no longer hear the voice of God and become susceptible to rebellion and disobedience. To understand or recognize His voice, and walk in fellowship with Him, we must live in holiness. I am not merely saying sinning will cause you to miss out on God's best as some say. I am saying sin can ultimately cause you to lose everything, including your soul. Sin has consequences, and the more you allow into your life, the more severe are those consequences. Again,

Satan is not just interested in keeping you from having God's best or being a mere hindrance or nuisance. His objective is to draw you into rebellion against God, leading to the same fate as his, which is eternal separation from God. Holiness is not a suggestion, nor a denomination. It is a mandate from God and stands between God's Kingdom and Satan's kingdom.

III. Prayer - Our lifeline to God.

Prayer is the difference between having a religious experience driven by emotion, or a genuine relationship with God inspired by faith. It is a decision to merely view God as a resource, or to see Him as a Father who orders our steps and guides us through life. Prayer is our opportunity to communicate with God and share intimate time and fellowship with Him.

Prayer is not a ritual but a lifestyle. We don't fit prayer into our lives; instead; we adjust our lives around prayer. This dates to the Garden of Eden when God spoke to Adam in the cool of the day. The same way He talked with Adam, teaching Him how to walk in His dominion and authority, sharing His thoughts with him, His love, and His character is the same way God wants to communicate with us. Prayer is our hotline and affords each of us equal opportunity and access to the throne of God regardless of education, ethnicity, environment, or finances.

Prayer is fueled by faith and not the wisdom of men. To effectively pray, we must believe that God is and that He is a rewarder of those who diligently seek Him. We must believe that He can do all things and we are entitled to His promises, not because of works we have done, but because of the covenant we have through the Blood of Jesus and lining up with His word. Most importantly, we must believe that God wants to honor His promises because of His unlimited, grace, mercy, and love.

Prayer is also a time for supplication, which means making our request and petitions to God and seeking Him for guidance and direction in every area of our life. He is our Heavenly Father, who knows all things, and never intended for us to go through this journey alone. His word tells us He will never leave nor forsake us; therefore; we ask with confidence, knowing

He will supply our every need according to His

purpose. Not only must we ask God (who already

knows our need), but we must have the patience to wait

on Him.

Philippians 4:6 "Be careful for nothing; but in every
thing by prayer and supplication with thanksgiving let
your requests be made known unto God."

Prayer is also a time for repentance and

confessing our misdeeds and shortcomings before God.

It is not just confessing our sins but seeking His

strength to turn away from them. As we stand before

His throne, there is power available to crucify the flesh

and overcome our wicked ways. He chastens us out of

love, letting us know where we deviated from the path.

As we stand before Him, He also ministers to our

weaknesses and shows us how to close the door that

allowed sin to enter our life. When we miss the mark,

prayer is our lifeline to remain in fellowship with God.

I John 1:8-10
1:8 "If we say that we have no sin, we deceive
ourselves, and the truth is not in us."
1:9 "If we confess our sins, he is faithful and just to
forgive us *our* sins, and to cleanse us from all
unrighteousness."

1:10 "If we say that we have not sinned, we make him a liar, and his word is not in us."

Prayer further includes confessing His Word back to Him and trusting His promises that He will bring it to pass. The Bible tells us there is power in agreement, and through prayer, we can come into agreement with God. You don't have to hunt down someone to agree with you when you have 24/7 access to the Word of God. A place we can come into agreement with God's will, release our faith in His word, and exercise our authority and dominion in the earth. Each day we are scripting the life God intended for us through confessing His word in prayer. Every area of our life should have a prayer script attached to it by confessing what the word of God says about it. Our marriage, our job, our finances, our family, and our relationships should all have a script we are confessing through faith.

Romans 4:17 "(As it is written, I have made thee a father of many nations,) before him whom he believed, *even* God, who quickeneth the dead, and calleth those things which be not as though they were."

Prayer is also a place of intercession, or standing in the gap for someone else. The Bible says there is no greater love than a man lay down his life for his brother. When we approach the throne of God, on behalf of our fellow man, we touch the very heart of God. Intercession involves many areas, some of which are family, the body of Christ, our nation, leaders, persecuted believers, the unsaved, revival in the land, for Israel, peace in Jerusalem, and for people to be prepared when He returns. The Holy Ghost will also use this space to confess the will of God through us. We talked earlier in this book about the awesome power of the Holy Ghost to intercede through us and the necessity for speaking in other tongues.

Romans 8:27 "And he that searcheth the hearts knoweth what *is* the mind of the Spirit, because he maketh intercession for the saints according to *the will of* God."

Prayer is also a place of warfare and coming against Satan and his kingdom of darkness. We cannot defeat Satan through natural means. Too many of us are relying on will power and positive thinking to win spiritual warfare. The battle is fought and won in the prayer closet where we clothe ourselves with the whole armor of God. We put on the helmet of salvation, having been redeemed by the Blood of Jesus from sickness, poverty, and death. We gird up our loins with truth by standing on the unadulterated word of God, which is a wall keeping us from those things we should not do and a guide, leading to those things we should. We put on the breastplate of righteousness and come into agreement with the character of Christ to be a source of light during darkness. Our feet are shod with the preparation of the gospel of peace, which gives us comfort in an unpredictable world full of anxiety, worry, and stress. We take hold of the sword of the spirit and rebuke the works of Satan according to the word of God coming against all principalities, powers, the rulers of the darkness of this world, and spiritual wickedness in high places. We grab the shield of faith which is our defense against all the lies, deception, and any other weapon, tool, device, tactic, or plan of Satan or man contrary to the will of God for our lives. In all things pertaining to this life, we look to the Holy Ghost for guidance and direction. It is the power of the Holy

Ghost that gives the wisdom to speak the mysteries of God, and the boldness to bombard the very gates of Hell.

II Corinthians 10:3-6
10:3 "For though we walk in the flesh, we do not war after the flesh:"
10:4 "(For the weapons of our warfare [are] not carnal, but mighty through God to the pulling down of strong holds ;)"
10:5 "Casting down imaginations, and every high thing that exalteth itself against the knowledge of God, and bringing into captivity every thought to the obedience of Christ;'
10:6 "And having in a readiness to revenge all disobedience, when your obedience is fulfilled."

In other words, we must trust God and be Battle Ready! **THE END**

The Battle Ready Conclusion Prayer

Personal Repentance

Praises be to the God of Abraham, Isaac, and Jacob, the Holy One of Israel, Alpha and Omega, the beginning and the end. From everlasting to everlasting, the only wise God. The all-powerful and all-knowing God who is full of love and compassion. The God who is longsuffering and patient and whose promises never fail. Dear Heavenly Father, I give you thanks and praise for your strength, your wisdom, and might, and I glorify your wonderful name. Your glory will not be given to another nor your praise to graven images. You alone are the God of the heavens above, the earth beneath, and the waters under the earth, and all power and authority belong to you.

Father, I thank you for sending your only begotten Son, My Lord and Savior Jesus Christ, the hope of my salvation, the King of Kings and Lord of Lords. He, who is highly exalted and given a name above all names. That at His glorious name every knee shall bow of things in heaven, things in the earth, and things under the earth; and every tongue shall confess that He is Lord.

I come before you Lord with a humble heart and transparent in my motives submitting my own life to the scrutiny of this prayer. I place my shortcomings and weaknesses at your throne, seeking your mercy and grace. In the name of Jesus and the power of His blood, please do not leave me to my own devices but save me from myself, for in this flesh dwelleth no good thing. Your word says we have all sinned and come short of your glory, so let your correction first begin with me. Let my heart be pricked, and my conscious stirred as I echo the words of the apostle Paul "that Christ Jesus came into this world to save sinners of whom I am chief." I stand before you Lord guilty as charged and grateful to receive your correction; for as many, as you love, you rebuke and chasten. I pray that you show me the error of my ways and teach me to walk according to your statutes so that I am not the least bit comfortable in sin, but rather sold out and surrendered to you. I pray

Lord that you remove the beam out of my eye so that I may see clearly to pray for others. For the good that I know to do, I don't always perform, and the evil that I despise sometimes gets the best of me. I pray that you wipe away my guilt and bless me with your peace; for you know my thoughts, the secrets of my ears, the trafficking of my eyes, and the conspiracies of my heart. Let not my faults fall into the hands of those that persecute me, nor let my weaknesses be on display. Deliver me Lord from the whisper of sin, every trace of deception, and the temptations and desires of the flesh. Let not my mind betray me, nor allow me to faint in the battle.

I confess Lord; I am guilty of leaving my first works, and my first love for I have been distracted by the world around me. I have been bombarded by sinful thoughts and have battled the desires within, failing to exercise discretion in what I see and what I hear. At times I have entertained evil in my heart and allowed bitterness to consume me. I have been lulled to sleep by complacency, slothfulness, and a lack of passion and desire. I repent Lord in the name of Jesus, and I turn

351

away from all sin and disobedience. Help me to forgive those who have offended me and please forgive me of my trespasses and cleanse me from all unrighteousness. Deliver me from all evil and wash me thoroughly from all iniquity. Crucify me daily so that I may walk after the examples of Christ and allow His light to shine in me. I plead the precious blood of Jesus over my life, and I pray that you strengthen me in my time of need. These things I ask in the name of Jesus. Amen

A Prayer for The Nation

In the name of Jesus and the power of His blood I come before you Gracious and kind God who knows the beginning and the end, whose compassion holds back judgment, and whose word is a double-edged sword, I boldly approach your throne. I come before you confessing your word that if we will humble ourselves and pray, seek your face, and turn from our wicked ways, then you will hear from Heaven, forgive our sins, and heal our land. I come before you Lord with a heavy heart petitioning you on behalf of the nation I love, for as a nation, we have fully turned away from following you. We had all but abandoned you while allowing every foul spirit to prosper and iniquity to abound. Lord, you blessed us with great riches and resources, expanded our borders, granted us might and protection, and caused us to be a beacon of light for all the nations of the world to see. Heavenly Father, we were once celebrated for our freedoms and opportunities, and despite our shortcomings, people came here from all over the world hoping for a better way of life. Now those same nations shall lament and weep for that great city sitting on many waters, for we have forsaken you God, the source of our strength and the secret behind our success. We have been unmindful and carelessly forgotten who formed us even transgressing your laws, changing your ordinances and breaking covenants.

Heavenly Father We have moved you to anger by placing other gods before you, blaspheming your name and doing exceedingly wicked things in your sight, rebelling against the very knowledge and fear of God. We disregard your instruction and have denied your name by foolishly turning away from your provision and protection. We have allowed corruption and greed to prosper, having no regard for the widow or the poor. We have fully served the god of this world resulting in rampant murder, immorality, abominations, divination, Baal worship, corruption, lawlessness, widespread violence and drug use, fornication, occultism, prostitution and human trafficking, a lack of natural affection, abortions, rebellious lifestyles, and the most perverse forms of spiritual adultery. We have come against your very design and plan, making a mockery of the family and the sanctity of marriage, while making every effort to erase the very memory of God from our institutions, schools, culture, and way of life. We refuse to give you glory and honor and have forgotten your great works. We arrogantly flaunt our exploits in your sight, and despite the visible signs of decay, collapse, and deterioration, we continue our course, refusing to change the error of our ways.

We have become a nation increasingly veering away from a genuine belief in God, Your statutes, and Your commandments and the same Christian morals and values that once made us a great nation are now seen as hateful and an infringement on the rights of others. Lord, we have forgotten that you are a righteous and Holy God who is not slack concerning His promises. In the name of Jesus and the power of His blood, I ask Lord for your mercy and forgiveness for the wrongs we have committed for it is our iniquities that separate us from your presence and our sins that cause us to be turned from your face. We stand in your courts guilty as charged and none is innocent before you. We have committed great transgressions, and we are not hiding from the consequences of our sins. You have called out to us, Lord, but we have not answered, you have given us instruction, but we have not taken heed. Your messengers have pleaded your case, but our ears are dull of hearing, and despite the evil that has come upon us we have not sought your face, nor have we turned from the errors of our ways; therefore we are judged and found guilty in your sight. We have whored after other gods and stood silent to the unrighteousness in the land. We have covered up our indiscretions, justified our sin, and given place to our fallen nature;

while enjoying the ungodly pleasures of this world. Please forgive us Lord for our hard and unrepented hearts. In the name of Jesus, we come before you Lord in humility for if we exalt ourselves or regard iniquity in our hearts, you will not hear us.

Lord look upon us for good and not evil and that we turn back to you and repent. In the name of Jesus and the power of His blood, I pray for revival and a great awakening in the land. I pray for leaders and all those that are in authority, our institutions and culture, and our people that we shall turn away from sin. For it is not your will that anyone perishes, but that we all come back to you. I pray that you're your anger and fury be turned away from our nation. I pray Lord that you remember your people that dwell within her borders and reserve your judgment for the ungodly and unjust. I pray Lord that we each search our hearts and make a personal commitment to repent, turn from our wicked ways and serve you, for you and only you are the God of our salvation.

A Prayer for The Church

In the name of Jesus and the power of His
Blood, I come before Lord recognizing that you are
supreme in authority, your power is great in the
Heavens and the earth, and that your anger is shown
against all wickedness and the evil imagination of men.
Father, I boldly approach your throne yet again, this
time asking for grace and mercy for your bride the
church. Your word says that judgment shall begin at the
house of God, so let the church bear the greatest
indictment. Because your invisible works are seen,
demonstrating your eternal power and divine nature, all
men are without excuse. Through hypocrisy, we have
given place to your enemies to blaspheme your great
and holy name. Because of our perversion and
deceitfulness, which brings shame to your name, they
question whether we are indeed your children. For this
cause, Lord, we are guilty and bear the more significant
burden. We have been weighed in the balance and been
found wanting, yet we refuse to change our path. We
have been deliberate in our great trespass before you

357

Lord, and we are not hidden from your sight. We have provoked you to anger with our foolish and unwise behavior being spiritually blind and naked, allowing the world to see our shame.

Heavenly Father, because you are a God of mercy and great compassion, we come before you in humility that you may examine our ways. We come before you confessing your word that if we humble ourselves and pray, seek your face, and turn from our wicked ways, then you will hear from Heaven, forgive our sins, and heal our land. In the name of Jesus and the power of His Blood, we thank you, Heavenly Father, that your hands are not shortened that they cannot save, nor your ear heavy that it cannot hear.

We stand before you Lord to answer the indictment that has been laid against us and pray that through repentance our sins will be forgiven for we have done wicked things in your sight even rebelling against your commandments, and your continued reminders and warnings.

In the name of Jesus, we acknowledge our shortcomings and weaknesses seeking to be washed in the Blood of our Savior, Jesus Christ. For we were called to be the salt of the earth, a people that would bear witness to your name, follow your examples, live by your commandments, and set a difference between that which is holy and that which is profane. Instead, our hearts have been pierced with the desires of the world, and we have adopted their ways, chasing after materialism and lust and compromising your standards. We have not sought you for who you are, but for what you can give and how much we can get. We have allowed worldliness into your church and created unholy alliances with the world calling that which is evil good and that which is good evil while refusing to take a righteous stand. We have sought validation from the world and coveted the admiration of men who have perverted your statutes for selfish gain. We have shown them all that is in your sanctuary, giving access to thieves and robbers, who now make merchandise of your sheep and a mockery of your name. We have failed to protect the innocent, neglected the cries of the poor, and watched as families are being destroyed. We have not sanctified you in the eyes of the people becoming powerless gift chasers who adorn the things on the outside while failing to address the evil within. We have compromised your word by seeking popularity and friendship with the world, choosing to entertain the masses with our talents and gifts while watering down your word and speaking fables instead of convicting people to change. We stand idle as the innocent are snatched from the womb while we defend the guilty, giving them a place on your stage. We are consumed with the pursuit of wealth, while at the same time, we are robbed of morality, dignity, and holiness. Through compromise and exploitation, we have lost our influence, through sermonettes and motivational speeches, we have catered to itching ears, and through hypocrisy and double standards, our pulpits have been stripped of power and authority. We have even embraced the lifestyles of this world and distorted the meaning of your love instead of preaching the sovereign design and plan of God. We have lost our way, Lord, and given over to the cares of this life. In the name of Jesus and the power of His Blood, forgive us, Father, for we bombard your throne with selfish prayers while the world around us declines in decay, drifting further and further away from you. We have been mesmerized by the lust of the world and desensitized by its influences while engaging in unspeakable acts; adultery and fornication, abortions, drunkenness, promiscuity, hatred and insensitivity, drug use, blasphemies, idolatry, man lying with man and women lying with women. We defile ourselves by flooding our minds with pornography, immorality and lust, and other kinds of sexual perversion. We have neglected our children and not taught them your ways and putting success and riches before love and direction. We have allowed our marriages to grow cold, harbored unforgiveness, and refused to show affection while opening the door for the enemy to wreak havoc in our families. We have become a lukewarm church lacking holiness and obedience to your Word, even denying your name Lord and abandoning the Cross. We have allowed false prophets to operate in the church while embracing false gods and religions. We are in a backslidden state and confess our sins before you. We were all born into this world with something to surrender, but so many of us have refused to let go choosing to embrace our fallen nature by making excuses for sin, as opposed to trusting your word for deliverance and healing. In doing so, we have denied the power of the Cross and the delivering authority of your resurrection. We go down in the water but never come up; sinking further and further into the death you gave your life to conquer. We have titles without meaning, performances without actors, services without substance, and buildings that are lifeless when it comes to the real power of God. In the name of Jesus and the power of His Blood, we repent and ask for your forgiveness. Lord, let your anger and fury be held back, and let your mercy fall upon us as we repent of our wicked deeds and turn back to you.

Let us once again be the people you have chosen to show yourself strong in the earth. That through our examples and trust in your word, the world will once again look to the church for salvation and demonstration of the real power of God. Lord, please hear our cry, incline thine ear, and behold our frail state that we may eagerly approach your throne with boldness and have confidence at your appearing. Your word says you will never leave or forsake us and we come to you by faith knowing that without faith it is impossible to please you.

Deliver us from the guilt of the past and wipe away all condemnation for through our sin, we have given the enemy access to our lives and the legal right to carry out his diabolical plan of destruction against us, but now Lord, through repentance, his rights have been revoked. In the name of Jesus, we denounce Satan and his demonic forces of evil and his rebellion against the Kingdom of God. In the name of Jesus and the finished work of the Cross, he loses all rights to torment, deceive, destroy, afflict, and manifest himself in the lives of your people, and we sever all ties, cooperation, agreement, conspiracy and relationship with the world and world system. In the name of Jesus and the power of His Blood, we command Satan to lose every stronghold, demonic manifestation, false belief, vice, grip, addiction, spell, and curse right now according to the word of God. We choose you Lord and the finished work of the Cross and want no part of Satan and the temptations of this world. I declare right now that we are loosed in your precious name.

Lord, we renew our covenant and commitment to you and exercise our choice to faithfully serve you with all our heart, mind, body, soul, and spirit. In the name of Jesus, we make a conscious choice to turn back to you and once again follow after your statutes and commandments and pledge our undivided service and devotion to you. For we have been brought with a price and serving you is our reasonable service. Please help us Lord to be lights in this world, ambassadors of the Most High God, and instruments of righteousness, representing your will and not our own.

I pray Lord that our hunger and thirst for you is never quenched and that you give us both to will and to do your good pleasure that we as a church may fulfill the calling and purpose that you have spoken over our lives. In the name of Jesus and the power of His Blood, we denounce the pleasures of this world, false doctrine and all forms of spiritual adultery, and pray that you expose the synagogue of Satan operating behind church walls, every lying and deceiving spirit, and demons operating as angels of light. Let us not worship or reverence anyone or anything but the true and living God, and drive out the spirit of antichrist. In the name of Jesus and the power of His Blood, I pray that you remove all doubts and bring revelation to every distortion of the truth and that we drive out the spirit of Jezebel that teaches fornication, lust, and idolatry. That her curse, seduction, and influence be broken and bound right now in the name of Jesus and erased from the hearts and minds of your people. I ask Lord that the depths of Satan operating in the church be exposed and driven out in Jesus' name. That we no longer defile ourselves through the lust of the flesh, and the pride of life hating all evil, pride, arrogance, and the evil way. Grant us spiritual discernment that we are not deceived. Let us examine the fruit of a man and not be gift chasers led astray by talents gifts, and charisma.

In the name of Jesus and the power of His Blood, I pray that the church will once again be known for its good works, love, faith, dedication, patience, and compassion to all men. That we hate the sin but love the sinner understanding that we have all fallen short of the glory of God. Let us love according to the word of God; standing on the truth, preaching the word in and out of season, and making no provision for the flesh, while understanding that grace is not an excuse for sin and a justification for Heaven.

Help us Lord to minister without compromise to those seeking the truth and be found without spot or wrinkle boldly proclaiming the truth of Christ and the power of His resurrection. Let us live and reign with Christ, clothed with holiness and abiding in His presence through eternity. In the name of Jesus and the power of His Blood, I speak life into your church and come against all dead things. Let our branches bring forth fruit in their season, and the waters of life nourish our roots. Let us be called and set apart, chosen and faithful, serving as kings and priest in your kingdom knowing that we are in the end times. That we are not lulled to sleep by the passing of days nor deceived by scoffers who deny your coming, but that we are watchful and that day does not overtake us as a thief in the night. We are pilgrims in the earth and this is not our home, so we look forward to the rapture and the second coming of Christ having faith that the promises of God shall come to pass. In the name of Jesus, I pray that we hold fast to our belief that you are the way, the truth, and the life, and that no man cometh to the Father but by you and that we never lose our boldness and passion for the Most High God.

In the name of Jesus and the power of His Blood, I pray that we are not weary in well doing and that we have a desire to spend quality time in your word and fellowship with you. That we do not neglect the fellowshipping of the saints as we are one in the body of Christ and sealed by the precious gift of the Holy Spirit. That we may all faithfully walk in the calling and purpose we have been given pressing toward the mark and high calling of Jesus Christ our Lord. I thank you Lord that you can keep that which we have committed unto you against that day and that nothing we have done is in vain, but all things are accounted to our Heavenly account that we may be rich towards God. Lord, let us run this race with patience looking unto you who has endured the Cross and despised the shame for the joy that was set before you. That our

367

name be confessed before the Father and written in the Lambs Book of Life. I pray Lord that we are steadfast and unmovable, always abounding in the love of God that we may receive a crown of life promised to those who endure until the end.

Now unto God who knows the beginning from the end, who is our shield in time of trouble, and who causes us to endure the fiery furnaces of life, we give you honor and praise. We proclaim and ascribe greatness to your name for your deeds are perfect, and all you do is just and fair. You own the cattle on a thousand hills and cause darkness to flee in the presence of light. I pray, Lord, that we demonstrate our gratitude for all you have done by keeping your commandments. For your word says obedience is better than sacrifice and rebellion is as the sin of witchcraft. Let your word be a light unto our path, revelation in darkness, and our blueprint for all matters pertaining to this life and the one thereafter.

It is through you Heavenly Father and the power of your might that one can chase a thousand and two can put ten thousand to flight, for greater is He that is in us than he that is in the world.

THE BATTLE-READY
CONCLUSION

JUDGMENT

Acknowledgments

Blue Letter Bible
www.blueletterbible.org

King James Version of the Bible used unless
otherwise noted

Gems From Joy Ministries

Rose City Community Church

Cover & Interior Design by
LaTanya Orr, iselah.com

ILJACMDBF

Special Contributor
Joy Hopson

Made in the USA
Middletown, DE
31 August 2019